GLADIATRIX

The
TRUE STORY OF HISTORY'S
UNKNOWN WOMAN WARRIOR

AMY ZOLL

BERKLEY BOULEVARD BOOKS, NEW YORK

Most Berkley Boulevard Books are available at special quantity discounts for bulk purchases for sales promotions, premiums, fund-raising, or educational use. Special books, or book excerpts, can also be created to fit specific needs.

For details, write: Special Markets, The Berkley Publishing Group, 375 Hudson Street, New York, New York 10014.

A Berkley Boulevard Book
Published by The Berkley Publishing Group
A division of Penguin Putnam Inc.
375 Hudson Street
New York, New York 10014

PRINTING HISTORY
Berkley Boulevard trade paperback edition / September 2002

Visit our website at www.penguinputnam.com

Library of Congress Cataloging-in-Publication Data

Zoll, Amy.
Gladiatrix : the true story of history's unknown woman warrior / Amy Zoll.
p. cm.
Includes bibliographical references.
ISBN 0-425-18610-5
1. London (England)—Antiquities, Roman. 2. Great Britain—History—Roman period, 55 B.C.–449 A.D. 3. Excavations (Archaeology)—England—London. 4. London (England)—History—To 1500. 5. Women soldiers—England—London. 6. Gladiators—England—London. 7. Boadicea, Queen, d. 62. 8. Women soldiers—Rome. I. Title.

DA677.1 .Z65 2002
936.2'103—dc21
2002021543

PRINTED IN THE UNITED STATES OF AMERICA

10 9 8 7 6 5 4 3 2 1

CONTENTS

PREFACE

L ondon in the late first century A.D., a thriving commercial center for the Roman territory of Britannia. It is a young city—only a single generation has passed since its founding along the banks of the Thames—but it represents all that the Roman Peace has to offer. Here are the hallmarks of civilization: a forum and basilica for the conduct of Roman business, law, and government, paved roads and public bathhouses, shops selling the exotic ware that arrive at London's bustling port from every corner of the empire.

On this day, however, the markets and wharves are quiet. Only a few stragglers haunt the forum plaza. Today, the city's heart belongs to its dazzling new amphitheater. The imposing timber and stone edifice dwarfs the houses around it, dominating the skyline. Its walls reverberate with the cheers of the thousands inside.

The sun is past its peak and, still, hundreds throng toward the stadium. They join many who have been there all day, not wanting to miss a moment's spectacle. But, as the shadows lengthen, anticipation grows. Everything up until now had been mere appetizer. The main events are about to begin.

In the shadowy tunnels beneath the stands, a group of warriors make their grim preparations. Soon, they will be called upon to fight each other for their very lives, but for now, they are comrades-in-arms: checking the fit of helmets and making peace with their far-flung gods. They are the gladiators.

One of their number stands apart, face pressed against the heavy wooden door to the arena, straining for a glimpse at the audience beyond. This does not go unnoticed by another, an older gladiator, sun-weathered and scarred by innumerable bouts. The veteran goes to reassure the anxious fighter.

"Hometown crowd, eh? They're always the best."

The younger combatant is unconvinced. "They weren't so happy with me when I left."

"Give them a good show and they'll forgive almost anything." A fanfare of horns blare outside. "Chin up. That's our cue."

Taking up arms and shields, the gladiators assemble. Light floods the corridor as the arena doors are thrown open. It's game time, and any trace of doubt is now gone from the young fighter's face as she steps out onto the field.

The crowd roars with surprise and delight. The sponsors had promised novelty and variety and they did not disappoint. Here before them was a woman warrior . . . a gladiatrix.

INTRODUCTION

From the romantic paintings of the nineteenth century to the epic films of the twentieth, the popular image of the Roman gladiator has been of a life bloody, brutal, and short. A timeless tragic hero, compelled to fight to the death by forces beyond his control, his fate ultimately resting in the hands of a capricious emperor and a bloodthirsty mob. He is noble, honorable, and invariably doomed. He is also a *he*. This powerful symbol of strength and resolve has always been decidedly male.

In September of 2000, experts at the Museum of London made an announcement that would challenge such long-held preconceptions. Not only did they believe they had identified the burial of a gladiator—an achievement in and of itself—but the fragmented remains had proven to be those of a woman.

The discovery caused a stir within traditional scholarship and garnered media attention worldwide. The find was unprecedented and its interpretation controversial, certainly, but this was not the first evidence for the existence of female gladiators. Brief mentions and oblique references can be teased out of the works of several ancient writers, while a relief in the British Museum indisputably depicts two such combatants, going so far as to identify them by name.

Why, then, did this latest discovery spark such public interest? Perhaps it comes at a time when, like the Romans two thousand years before, there is a more receptive audience for strong feminine images. Where the Romans had the legend of the Amazons and Boudica, the Celtic warrior queen, we now cheer professional female athletes competing in sports once considered the exclusive domain of men and follow the exploits of fictional heroines like Xena: Warrior Princess on television.

In her time, however, the gladiatrix represented the epitome of social contradiction. Even her male counterparts, while highly celebrated and capable of achieving great fame in their lifetimes, were considered to be of the lowest status imaginable, akin to slaves, even if they had been born free citizens. A woman who fought in the arena not only went against Roman cultural mores but exploded gender definitions as well.

Difficulties reconciling the conflicts inherent in her life may be reflected in the death of the mysterious woman discovered by the Museum of London team. The contents of her grave and the care taken in its preparation suggest she was a woman of some renown, possibly high rank. Yet, she was laid to rest in relative obscurity, not among the monuments and mausolea of Roman London's notables, but out along the periphery with those of more questionable standing.

The quality and quantity of items contained in the grave—an assemblage without parallel in Britain—may allude to the beliefs of the deceased and the rituals performed at her graveside. There are the remains of a sumptuous funeral feast, including such imported delicacies as dates, almonds, and figs. Eight ceramic incense burners and the remains of burnt pinecones suggest a ceremony heavy with exotic scent. Even the cones themselves were rarities, coming from the stone pine (*Pinus pinea*), a species not indigenous to the area, but closely associated with the rites of the Roman amphitheater.

Also found among these goods, eight small pottery lamps, four of a type produced in Gaul and not often seen in Britain. Of these, one depicts a fallen gladiator, possibly a direct reference to the person being honored. Three others bear the likeness of the jackal-headed Anubis, Egyptian god of the dead and conveyor of souls to the underworld.

How did this enigmatic woman come to rate such an eclectic and worldly collection of artifacts? Why did she receive such a reverential but, at the same time, ignominious burial? Curators at the Museum of London argue that few career paths were available to women that could have brought them exposure to cosmopolitan ideas and obvious personal success, yet keep them at the fringes of society: She was a gladiatrix.

Celebrities and outcasts, gladiators enjoyed great admiration and rewards, but risked paying the ultimate price. What would drive a woman to such extremes? This book will explore the little-known world of the gladiatrix: the evidence for her existence, the history and legends that may have given her rise, her life training for combat in the arena, and the bloody spectacle of the Roman amphitheater in which she could well have met her end.

Camilla stepped out into the light of the arena. As if she needed another reminder of where she was, the sun felt different here. In the Mediterranean lands where she had trained and fought, the heat hit like a wall and quickly made armor burn to the touch. Here it gently warmed her back after the dank coolness of the amphitheater tunnel. This was the sun of home.

Possibly the only familiar thing about the place. Much had changed in the years since she had left. Of course, at the time, London had been little more than a smoking ruin and she had been accused of helping make it so. Since then, its inhabitants seem to have busied themselves with turning this remote outpost of the empire into a poor copy of a proper Roman town.

And how many of her countrymen, Camilla wondered, looking out at the sea of faces, had turned themselves into poor copies of proper Romans? Were they all now falling over themselves to speak a foreign tongue and live in square houses just for the right to drape themselves in bedsheets and swear allegiance to an unseen emperor?

In the distance, she could barely make out the women spectators, uppermost in the stands, laughing and waving the hems of their dresses as they would for male gladiators. If things had been different, had she stayed, would she have been among them, satisfied to be relegated to the back of the crowd?

Agave danced past, leaping and whooping, playing up to the audience, the moth-eaten leopard's skin tied about her shoulders flapping behind her. The display brought even louder cheers as the small troupe marched around the ring.

Those who had made a day of the games had already been treated to the usual execution of prisoners and animal hunt. Camilla had seen the sad excuse for a lion backstage—the creature had not traveled well, but Rufus was probably back there right now negotiating for its mangy hide to complete Heraklia's outfit.

She spotted the veteran fighter ahead of her. Although she was trying hard to conceal it, Camilla could tell Heraklia was limping.

"That leg's still bothering you," she said, catching up. "You should've had Rufus pull you from the lineup."

Heraklia laughed. They both knew the company's owner better than that. "Are you kidding, and ruin his big break?"

Rufus had been contracted to provide five fighting pairs for this prestigious—if backwater—event and damned if he wasn't going to take women off the street and put swords in their hands to do it.

Although only a few years older than Camilla, Heraklia had had a sword in her own hand by the time most girls were starting to weave their wedding veils. She was so close to retirement now she could taste it. Nothing was going to jeopardize that, not even an injury.

"You worry too much. Today's like any other day—we live or we die."

Somehow, Camilla failed to be reassured by this sentiment. But it was not until they turned to salute the games' sponsor that she realized how very wrong her friend's words had been.

Today was not like any other day, for staring down at Camilla from the stands was her own father.

1

DISCOVERY

Who was the mystery woman buried in an unmarked grave on the outskirts of Roman London? Laid to rest with great reverence and ceremony, her burial contained a rich and remarkable array of artifacts, yet it was deliberately set apart from other graves of its stature. Did this seclusion reflect the woman's status? Had she been an outsider in life as well as in death? Who among those on society's periphery would have merited such a lavish and ritualized funeral? These were the questions facing members of the Museum of London Archaeological Service when, during a routine excavation, an extraordinary discovery was made.

In a city as rich in history as London, it is sometimes difficult to put spade to ground *without* turning up some discarded relic of the past: a bit of pottery or broken brick, a centuries-old house foundation, a forgotten road. For nearly two thousand years, people have made their homes along this bend in the River Thames, building and rebuilding on the same piece of real estate. The process continues today, only now archaeologists work in advance of development, protecting and preserving ancient remains that lie under constant threat from the backhoes and bulldozers of progress.

London's dense settlement and continuous development have left their marks both aboveground and below. On the surface, the signs are easy to spot. The Tower of London and Westminster Abbey, centerpieces of the medieval landscape, still draw legions of visitors daily, while many streets in the city center follow the courses of earlier Roman roads and respect the invisible line of long demolished town defenses. Beneath the tower blocks and motorways, however, the evidence is far from clear. Archaeologists are confronted with a muddle of crisscrossing remnants of lives lived, layer upon layer, each successive occupation intercutting and obscuring the last. Through their efforts, London's long history is taking shape, but gradually, pieced together from glimpses when land is laid bare in preparation for yet more construction.

The story of London begins in earnest in A.D. 43 when the forces of the emperor Claudius poured across the Channel and set about conquering the island in characteristic Roman fashion. The imperial army, intent on securing a foothold in the southeast, built forts and defenses, established lines of communication and supply, and soon set their sights on the native stronghold of Camulodunum (modern Colchester) as the first step in the subjugation of the local populace. To aid in this objective, a bridge was built spanning the Thames, not far from where London Bridge now stands.

Camulodunum fell later that same year and became the site of

the first Roman colony in the new province, settled by retired soldiers. Elsewhere, other less official centers also began to spring up
as traders and entrepreneurs followed in the wake of the conquerors, attracted by new opportunities in a new land. London was
their greatest success story. Ideally situated to exploit the principle
north-south routes of the time, this settlement grew quickly along
the north shore of the river.

During its early years, London's development reflected its status
as an unofficial frontier town. Rectangular timber-framed buildings
mingled with traditional roundhouses, the circular thatched huts
used by the native inhabitants. By A.D. 60, however, this mercantile
community must have seemed a sufficient reminder of the hated
Roman occupation for it to be razed by neighboring tribes when
they rose in a brief but devastating mass revolt. In the last decades
of the first century A.D., London managed to emerge reborn from
its own ashes, acquiring many of the features of a true Roman city,
including a forum, amphitheater, and even its own suburbs.

In the fall of 1996, a team led by Anthony Mackinder from the
Museum of London Archaeological Service had the task of investi-
gating a block along Great Dover Street in the Southwark district
of Greater London slated to become new student housing for the
Guy's and St. Thomas' Hospital Trust. What they uncovered would
enrich our understanding of the city's formative years and shed light
on some of its less well-known—but perhaps most celebrated—residents.

The site, dubbed "165 Great Dover Street" for the address of
one of the buildings along the street's frontage, presented all the
typical challenges that beset the urban archaeologist. The Museum

of London team had just a few short months to evaluate an enormous area, covering upward of eight thousand square meters, before the heavy-duty earthmovers gouged into the ground and removed any traces of the past.

Archaeological excavation is, by design, a painstaking and laborious process, for the very act of investigation, however meticulous, will destroy the original state of a site. Archaeologists must therefore exercise tremendous care not to overlook even the most subtle and ephemeral of evidence—from stains in the soil left by long-decayed wood posts to tiny seeds to microscopic pollen grains—all of which can provide important clues in the final analysis. In a constantly changing, built-up environment such as London, however, the drive is always to dig deeper to build higher. As a result, difficult choices must sometimes be made. For those archaeologists involved in "rescue" operations, where a site is in imminent danger of destruction, the desire to mount a complete and thorough investigation is tempered by the knowledge they have only a limited time in which to learn all they can from a location before it is lost forever.

Prior to undertaking any full-scale excavation, the history of the lot on Great Dover Street was researched and the land tested to determine where best to focus the team's energies. Some sections could be quickly ruled out from further consideration. Along the west side of the tract, the building for which the site was named and the smaller brick buildings flanking it were not scheduled for demolition, so no action needed to be taken there. On the east side, bounded by Tabard Street, deep basements sunk as part of postwar development had already obliterated any archaeological remains, as had construction on Black Horse Court at the south end of the site.

Based on these assessments, the decision was made to concentrate efforts on the northwest corner of the area, where the chances for finding intact deposits were greatest.

Even with the size of the study area much reduced, the team soon had their hands full. It was not long before they realized they had happened upon the outer edge of an extensive Roman cemetery. Based upon the objects recovered, the burial ground had been in active use during the early centuries of the period. In this small corner alone, the remains of more than thirty individuals were found, many solitary interments, others part of larger mortuary complexes.

Men, women, and children were laid to rest here along a stretch of old Watling Street, a main north-south thoroughfare of the time. Roman custom did not allow burial within city walls, so it was common for *necropoli*—cities of the dead—to grow just outside the gates. The approaches to the east, west, and north of Roman London, or Londinium as it was then known, had once all been crowded with polished stone monuments, inscribed with the names and achievements of deceased notables, each vying for the attention of passersby.

Although located clear across the Thames, the growth of a funerary complex in north Southwark echoes the area's own rise as the southern gateway to Londinium. Originally composed of a number of broad sandy islands set in marshy terrain, this shore had only ever been sparsely inhabited prior to the Roman conquest. Despite its low-lying geography, the Southwark islands provided the narrowest crossing point in the immediate area and the Romans wasted no time in establishing this vital link. Once the bridge was constructed, many of the major arteries leading to and from points south came to converge in Southwark, and settlement at this important crossroads began as early as A.D. 50. Southwark's history became inextricably tied with that of the city on the opposite bank. It seems to have shared in London's fate only a scant decade later, when British tribes rebelled against their Roman oppressors and set the city alight. Across the river, recent excavations have revealed a corresponding horizon of burnt material—the charred timber and mud walls of fallen buildings—suggesting the Southwark settlement was not spared the torch.[1]

Throughout the Roman period, occupation in Southwark clustered around the bridgehead on the north island, the largest of the river islands. The exact boundaries of the settlement are difficult to determine, as they tended to shift over time, but it is likely that the expansive burial ground that developed just to the south of the islands would have been situated along the settlement's fringes. Together, the numerous graves and mortuary monuments form a larger funerary zone that rivals in extent, if not density, those found directly outside the gates of Londinium. The site of 165 Great Dover Street lies on the southeastern edge of this community of the dead.

The 165 Great Dover Street excavation was located about a kilometer southeast of the Roman bridge along Watling Street. Originating on the Kent coast, the line of Watling Street in Southwark is believed preserved by present-day Tabard Street.[2] Indeed, excavation quickly revealed a section of a broad avenue, graveled and graded in typical Roman manner, paralleling Tabard and demarcating the eastern extent of the study area.

When the course of Watling Street was laid out in the mid–first century A.D., the surrounding countryside seems to have been mostly open farmland. Ghostly impressions left in the soil attest to the land's initial use. A series of ditches, running parallel and perpendicular to the road, may have served as agricultural field boundaries. The function of a large wooden structure that stood amidst the ditchwork, however, is unknown. All that remained when its presence was detected in the site's earliest occupation level was a rectangular set of pits where its upright wooden posts had once stood. The building, though substantially constructed, appears to have been short-lived, having been purposefully demolished when the plot was given over to funerary use.

The construction of a small stone building at the end of the first century A.D. marks the beginning of the site's transformation. The square masonry structure was either a shrine or a mausoleum designed to emulate the plan of a Romano-Celtic temple, an architectural type well-known from Britain and other western Roman provinces. Thought to reflect a fusion of ideals of the Mediterranean world and local Iron Age peoples, these buildings consisted of a central roofed chamber, or *cella*, bounded by a walled precinct. The open area within the walls of the Great Dover Street example contained a stone-lined well, likely intended for ritual use, as well as the base for a tombstone or altar. A small group of associated burials was also found set close behind the *cella* in the space between it and the surrounding curtain wall.

Around this same time, an unenclosed and seemingly unremarkable graveyard began to develop on the patch of ground set back from the road, just north of the temple-like building. Over the course of a few decades, the frontage along this section of Watling Street would become an upscale neighborhood for the dear departed, lined with individually walled family cemeteries, funerary monuments, and mausolea decorated with fine carvings and imported stone. Behind these more impressive memorials, however, the small graveyard continued to attract a much humbler clientele.

The final resting places of those interred in this plot must have been poorly marked, if at all. Later burials were found cutting into earlier ones, churning up the earth and the bones of previous occupants along with it. Several skeletons were found truncated and incomplete, while random remains turned up in the backfill of other burials. One man seems to have been disposed of in a particularly haphazard fashion. He was found facedown with one arm outstretched, as though his body had been tossed or dragged into its poorly dug grave. Few others in this graveyard were buried in coffins or with artifacts.

In such modest surroundings, archaeologists were astonished to come upon one burial that differed so dramatically from the rest that it would defy comparison. It was filled with a generous assortment of grave goods, and the body had been carefully prepared in a rare cremation process. Although the objects accompanying the deceased spoke of wealth and status, it quickly became clear these were the bones of no ordinary affluent citizen.

The unusual location of the grave was just the first of many curious aspects of this discovery. Somewhat removed from the rest, it was so far to the north that it nearly fell outside the study area. Nick Bateman, an archaeologist with the Museum of London Archaeological Service, recalls:

> It did at first appear from the reports that were coming from the
> excavation that the burial was actually in a quite different context

to the other burials there, and more particularly that it was isolated, by itself, but in fact the Dover Street burial, although to some extent peripheral, was indeed part of the whole cemetery complex.

A part of the cemetery, yet apart, the burial did not fit at all comfortably among the paupers but was physically segregated from the local leading lights in their roadside crypts. Another archaeologist with the Service, Jenny Hall, notes the apparent contradiction:

There was a walled cemetery with a possible mausoleum, but this burial was actually beyond that, outside the area. Now, if you've got someone who's wealthy and influential and part of Roman society, you would expect them to be buried in the walled cemetery, perhaps with their own mausoleum.

Although no standing monument or memorial appears to have been erected to mark the burial's location, the deceased had been given an extraordinary send-off. The body had been cremated on an elaborate type of funeral pyre known as a *bustum*. Usually reserved for the death of an important individual, there are only about twenty known examples of this custom from Britain.[3] The *bustum* was a uniquely Roman practice and consisted of a large rectangular pit overtop of which was built a substantial wooden platform. Distinguishing it from ordinary cremation techniques, the *bustum*'s underlying hollow improved airflow and kept the slowly descending tiers of the platform from smothering the blaze as they burned and fell. The wooden superstructure served the dual purpose of supporting the body as the flames consumed it, while at the same time fueling those flames. At one end of the pit at Great Dover Street, stake holes could still be seen, remnants of the pyre's stabilizing posts.[4] As they were reduced to ashes, the pyre and its contents would have dropped into the pit, where the remains would have been covered over with earth after the fires were spent.

Experiments conducted by forensics expert Jacqueline McKinley have shown that such a configuration would have burned very efficiently, producing high temperatures and a steady rate of consumption over many hours. An intense, sustained heat, at times reaching one thousand degrees centigrade, would have been hot enough to burn away muscle and fat, melt copper and even glass, but not quite sufficient to incinerate an entire corpse. Under such conditions, skeletal material shrinks and twists and changes color, bone fractures and becomes highly friable, but some amount is still recognizable. McKinley explains:

> It's a bit of a fallacy with cremated remains in that everything sort of disappears to a dust, or an amorphous blob. What actually happens is that you're oxidizing and dehydrating the body so all the organic components of the body, the soft tissues and the organic components of the bone, which is about 30 percent, are being burnt away, and you are going to be left with the inorganic components of the bone.

The inferno of the pyre had reduced the body in the Great Dover Street *bustum* to a confused jumble of hundreds of fragile and splintered bone fragments. Weighing a mere one kilogram in total, the pieces were carefully collected and sent back to the museum laboratories for analysis.

Just as intriguing as the body's location and treatment were the goods that accompanied it: items drawn from far and wide, consciously selected for their ritual significance. Some showed signs of having joined the deceased on the funeral pyre, while others had been added to the assemblage afterward. Together, they hinted at a lengthy and involved graveside ceremony.

In addition to the charred skeletal fragments, the burial also yielded a startling array of other organic matter. Some seventy liters of soil were collected from the fill of the *bustum* pit and sifted using a technique known as flotation. The process employs water to separate lighter particulates that may be mixed in with the soil but are so small they might otherwise be missed by standard excavation methods. In this manner, archaeobotanist John Giorgi and faunal analyst Kevin Rielly were able to identify a wide range of carbonized plant and animal remains: leftovers from an elegant meal.

Evidence for figs, dates, white almonds, barley, and several varieties of wheat were all found among the charred wood and earth. None of these ingredients, save for the cereal grains and possibly the figs, could have been grown locally and had to be imported from more southerly climes at some expense. Fig trees may have been introduced to Britain by this time, as their seeds are plentiful in other Roman period deposits, but this was the first instance in which a portion of the actual fruit had been preserved. The fruit and seeds of the dates found here also represented a first for a London excavation.

Along with these rare and exotic fruits and nuts, the bones of what appears to have been a whole butchered chicken and portions of another bird, perhaps a dove, were also recovered. These showed burn patterns that suggest the feast was intended to be symbolically enjoyed by the deceased alone, having been placed uncooked on the funeral platform with the body.

Other objects were almost completely devoured by the flames, leaving only the faintest of traces behind. Flecks of gold could be discerned in the soil samples, all that was left of some richly made textile, possibly a garment. Burnt and corroded iron nails implied the presence of a coffin or other container for offerings. Fragments of fire-distorted glass from one or more small bottles were also found melted by extreme heat. Glass vessels of this size often held sweet-smelling unguents that may have been used in the preparation of the body.

Scent, it seems, played a very important role in this funerary ritual. In addition to the remains of the food offerings, the pit's fill was littered with the remnants of numerous pinecones. These were identified as all coming from the same species of tree, the stone pine. Although such cones may have been consumed as a high-status food item, they were also frequently used as incense and are present in a number of ritual and religious contexts, including at the Vestal Virgins compound at the Forum in Rome.[5]

Like many of the foodstuffs found in the grave, the stone pine was originally native to the Mediterranean and later introduced to Britain with Roman occupation. According to Damian Goodburn, a specialist in ancient woods and woodworking with the Museum of London, there was only one place this species was growing in Britain at the time of the Great Dover Street burial: directly outside the London amphitheater.[6] The tall, fragrant trees were frequently planted around the exterior of amphitheaters to provide shade for the masses while its cones were burned as incense to mask the stench of blood and gore from the arena. The presence of their cones provides a direct link between the grave's occupant and the world of gladiators, according to Nick Bateman:

> The interesting thing is that we know that stone pine was used extensively for incense and we know that what went on in the amphitheater was intensely ritualized. There was an elaborate series of preparatory and concluding rituals and it's almost certain that the burning of incense was an essential part of it.

Eight small ceramic lamps had also been set at various points in the pit. Vessels of this type were ubiquitous throughout the Roman world, the ancient equivalent of modern lightbulbs, although they did not emit anywhere near the same amount of light. Mass-produced from multipart reusable molds, their basic components consisted of an enclosed round reservoir for holding oil and a tapering spout from which a wick would generate a tiny, flickering flame. Although a common form, the white clay used in the lamps found at Great Dover Street indicate that they had been imported to Britain from manufacturing centers in Rome's Gallic provinces. All had originally been dipped in a dark coating that, after firing, ranged in color from a rusty orange to a dark gray, possibly meant to mimic similar lamps fabricated from terra-cotta or bronze.

Of these eight lamps, four are undecorated. Although identical in style, these "factory lamps," or *Firmalampen*, appear to have been formed in different molds, with varying degrees of care taken in their execution. The other four lamps are of a volute type, with scrollwork at the spout and a raised figural design on the flat discus that makes up the top of the oil reservoir. The choices of subject matter on these vessels provide the strongest clues as to the identity of the grave's occupant.

Three lamps bear depictions of the Egyptian god Anubis, his jackal head shown in profile with its distinctive long pointed ears and snout. In these small, schematic representations, he wears a short, knee-length kilt or tunic and in his left hand he carries a wand or herald's caduceus, a symbolic attribute of the Roman deity Mercury. It was not uncommon in the ancient world for the divinities of one civilization to be adopted by another. Mercury himself had long become synonymous with the Greek deity Hermes. Both were messengers of the gods and conveyors of souls through the underworld, much like Anubis himself. Indeed, the close association between Hermes and Anubis is reflected in the Greek tradition by the composite deity Hermanubis.[7]

According to Andrea Wardle, finds specialist for the Museum of London, the choice of subject matter on these three nearly identical lamps was deliberate, perhaps referring to the occasion of the funeral itself or else some aspect of the deceased's own life.[8] Whether the presence of Anubis directly connects this individual with the cult of Isis, a popular Egyptian-inspired faith at the time, is a matter of some debate, however. Anubis' divine counterparts, Hermes and Mercury, also loomed large in the highly ritualized world of the arena and the lamps' motifs could be seen to allude in some way to the life and death struggles of gladiators, especially in light of the fourth picture lamp found in the grave.

The image on the final lamp is that of a fallen gladiator. The fighter wears the crested helmet and armament characteristic of the Samnite type.[9] Still grasping his sword, he is shown at the moment of defeat, collapsing backward with left arm upraised, either to

shield himself from his unseen opponent's killing blow or to plead
for mercy from the crowd. Gladiators, too, had close conceptual ties
to the underworld. Their origins can be traced back to early funerary rites in which combatants would battle to the death to prove
themselves worthy to escort departed aristocrats through the land
of the dead. Later, much of the symbolism underlying these acts was
retained in the arena even after their funereal associations were lost.

All of the lamps, both plain and decorated, were found broken
but complete or nearly complete, indicating they had been placed
whole into the grave. Not only were they intact, but they had been
brand-new as well. Lamps of this sort typically became darkened
and sooty at the spout where the wick guttered, but none showed
such telltale signs of use. This suggests they had been selected for a
symbolic purpose, perhaps intended to light the way for the
deceased in the afterlife. An expert on Roman lamps, Hella Eckhardt
found not only the types but the number of lamps remarkable:

> In Roman Britain, it is very unusual to find multiple lamps in a
> burial. Normally I'd expect to see one, maybe two lamps, but to
> find eight is unique and outstanding.

Based on the manufacture dates of the various forms, Eckhardt
was able to provide a date for the burial itself. Picture lamps such as
those found here entered the British repertoire around A.D. 20, pre-
ceding the Roman invasion by more than two decades. They
became increasingly less common after the province had been
established, petering out after the first century. Importation of the
undecorated lamps, on the other hand, did not begin until around
A.D. 70. The waxing and waning of these two types suggest that the

burial most likely took place at the point at which their periods of popularity overlap and both were widely available, around A.D. 70 or 80.

Eight ceramic *tazze*, open pedestaled containers believed used for the burning of incense, were also found in the grave, either directly on top of or in close association with the lamps. These vessels probably held the smoldering cones of the stone pine, but their contents had been spilled out among the ashes when most were set on the pit floor intentionally inverted. Although these vessels varied somewhat in size, all were strikingly similar in form and decoration. Each had a flaring frilled rim, a pattern repeated lower on the body just above where it began to taper to the base. All had been thrown on a potter's wheel and were made of a local clay known as Verulamium Region White. This material was named for the commercial pottery workshops that grew up along Watling Street south of the Roman town of Verulamium (modern St. Albans in Hertfordshire). Production began at this center shortly after the Roman conquest in A.D. 43 and was at its peak between A.D. 70 and 120.[10]

Tazze were not unknown from burials in Britain during this time, but like the lamps, it was extraordinary to find so many in a single grave: Until the Great Dover Street discovery, only twelve such vessels had been recovered from all four of London's cemeteries combined.[11] Similar to the lamps, these *tazze* do not appear to have seen heavy use prior to being committed to the earth. They were used at least once, however, as the interiors of most were sooted and charred. The irregular pattern of scorch marks, rising up along one side to the rim, suggests they were lit outside, where the prevailing winds caused their burning contents to lap against the vessel wall.[12]

Both the lamps and the *tazze* show no indication of exposure to the heat of the pyre, but rather had been carefully arranged on the floor of the *bustum* pit, possibly as offerings left by the mourners to mark the completion of the memorial service. Most of the cremated human remains were found beside or beneath one of the upturned *tazze*. They had been gathered up and redeposited after the embers grew cold: the final act in a complex funeral rite.

Grave goods of such exceptional quality and quantity attest to the care and respect with which this individual was laid to rest. Why, then, was the grave itself so anonymous? If this person had been a prominent member of the community, why were they not commemorated in a more permanent fashion or buried with the other members of their affluent and influential family? These are questions pondered by Nick Bateman:

> Obviously one starts to speculate. Why is this so? Why have we got this pretty elaborate rich burial ceremony going on? That speculation, to some extent, starts to fuel the idea of social exclusion. Is this person deliberately being excluded from the normal burial area?

In the rigid class system of Roman society, those of the lowest caste included slaves, criminals, and prostitutes. Their burials would have echoed their outsider status and been relegated to the fringes of the cemetery. None, however, would have been mourned in such a refined and costly manner as was the case at Great Dover

Street. Only one group among such outcasts would have been able to overcome deeply ingrained social stigma to achieve great wealth and renown: the gladiators.

But, if this was a gladiator, she was female: a gladiatrix. That was the stunning revelation to come from osteologist Bill White, who performed the initial assessment of the human remains from the Great Dover Street *bustum*. Although the material recovered hardly comprised a complete skeleton, portions of the pelvis, a key indicator of gender, were found sufficiently intact to make a definitive determination. A woman's pelvic bones tend to be wider and more bowl-shaped to facilitate childbirth, while a man's are larger and slightly more vertically oriented. White concluded that this individual was undoubtedly female.

Shortly after the pronouncement, however, the pelvic fragments and some other bones that had been separated from the rest for study were packed away. They have since been mislaid amidst the tens of thousands of other similar boxes stored in the Museum of London's vast warehouse. To date, Great Dover Street woman's missing pelvis has yet to be rediscovered, but the rest of her remains were kept on public display at the museum and were available to be reexamined by White and McKinley several years later.

From the pile of fragments and scraps, they were able to pick out a few bones that provided further information about the woman's age and stature. Vertebrae were small, even allowing for shrinkage during cremation, suggesting she may have been slight of build. Her bones appeared fairly mature, but showed no signs of degenerative diseases common among Roman populations as today, such as osteoarthritis. From this, they were able to estimate her age at death as somewhere around thirty years old. Slender and healthy, in the prime of her life, Great Dover Street woman captured the popular imagination, as well as that of the archaeologists responsible for bringing her to light. Jenny Hall remembers:

> People then started saying well, what have we got here, could we possibly have a female gladiator? That really made everyone go: no, can't, don't believe that. But when you sort of looked at all the facts you realized that it was a possibility, that this could be something really quite amazing.

Camilla's blood ran cold. Had he seen her? Did he recognize her?

Then she remembered her helmet. Hidden behind its ornate visor, there was no way her father could know her. She was just one of the anonymous women standing before the sponsor's box, ready to fight and die for his amusement.

Captured, sold into slavery, forced to become a gladiatrix . . . after all these years, she thought she was at least free of him. A lifetime ago, when Roman soldiers had dragged her through the streets and declared her a rebel and a traitor, he had not stepped forward to claim her as his own. With his silence, he had condemned her. Whether out of cowardice or ambition, she never knew—until now.

The man who had been her father descended into the arena with his entourage. Laughing and joking amongst themselves, they went through the motions of checking the combatants' weapons, vouching for their sharpness to an expectant audience.

He was so close, Camilla could reach out and touch the hem of his toga. Her breath caught as he stepped in front of her. She dumbly handed him her sword for inspection. Surely, he could see her heart pounding in her chest. That was, after all, where his eyes were pointed. But, after testing the weapon's edge, he passed it back without comment and he and his guests returned to their awning-shaded seats.

She was shaking. This was no good. She couldn't afford to lose focus, not now—her life depended on it.

When the lots were drawn, she nearly missed her name being called. To her relief, she had not been selected to come up against Heraklia this time. Camilla knew her friend and mentor's fighting style so well that the two could trade blows for an hour and the audience would be none the wiser. Today, though, she was too rattled to pretend at swordplay and make it look real. This time, it was going to be real.

She had been paired with Myrine instead. She was the new girl who had appeared on their doorstep the moment they arrived in London, begging to join the troupe. She came with her own equipment, all the best, highly polished and without a dent. And, of course, she had taken the name of a famous Amazon queen. Why did they always fancy themselves Amazon queens?

This pampered little gladiatrix-wanna-be was about to get much more than she bargained for. . . .

2

GODDESSES, AMAZONS, AND WARRIOR QUEENS

Evidence for the existence of gladiatrices is tantalizingly rare. This paucity has led some scholars to consider them a novelty act, an infrequent addition intended to spice up the usual fare for an increasingly jaded audience. However, the casual way in which references to female gladiators pepper both the historical and archaeological record suggests the practice may have been more widespread than direct evidence might otherwise indicate.

The poet Statius mentions a gladiatorial contest staged by the emperor Domitian in A.D. 88 in which the performances of women recalled the legends of the Amazons.[1] In his biography of the emperor, Suetonius describes this same event, noting that the women fought at night by torchlight.[2] As mortal combat was usually saved for last in the amphitheater's running order, it is possible these women were among the day's main attractions, rather than a mere sexual sideshow.

This does not mean their appearances were without controversy or social onus, however. Often, historians of the time raise the subject of women fighters as a means of emphasizing the debauched nature of an emperor's regime, especially in the cases of Nero and Domitian. Tacitus observes with distaste that during one year in Nero's reign the number of "distinguished women" who disgraced themselves in the arena exceeded "all precedent."[3] In a collection of epigrams by Martial celebrating the shows of the Colosseum in Rome, the poet makes reference to Domitian's insatiable appetite for spectacle involving participants of both sexes:

> It is not enough that warrior Mars serves you in unconquered arms, Caesar. Venus herself serves you too.[4]

It was the social class of these female fighters that appears to have been the cause of particular concern among ancient writers. The fact that noble women, whether coerced or (seemingly more often than not) willingly, engaged in this kind of public display was perhaps the most noteworthy aspect for many contemporary authors. Male gladiators, while much celebrated, were considered the lowest of the low, on par with slaves, prisoners, and criminals, from whose ranks they were often drawn. A woman of high status who would degrade herself in this way must have shocked and offended her peers.

When Eppia, the wife of a Roman senator, threw over her respectable life to run off with her gladiator lover, the poet Juvenal used her example to launch into a scathing review of the female gender. "What was it she saw in him," he asks, "that would compensate for her being called a gladiatrix?"[5] This was, apparently, the absolute depths to which a highborn lady could fall.

As a result of her scandalous affair, Eppia risked being mistaken for a *ludia*. The Romans, it seems, did not employ a feminized form of "gladiator" to refer to women who fought. Instead, in the few possible instances where this profession is mentioned by name, *ludia* is used. This somewhat ambiguous term is nonetheless telling as to the regard in which the gladiatrix was held.

Ludia is most commonly translated as "actress." Like its masculine counterpart, *ludio*, it is derived from the Latin *ludere*, meaning to play, mimic, deceive, or ridicule. Those who made their livelihood on the stage were considered to be extremely low-class. For Romans, using one's body to earn money was fundamentally distasteful, putting thespians on par with prostitutes and, of course, gladiators. Most actors were slaves or freedmen brought over from the eastern parts of the empire and especially Greece, the original source of inspiration for much of Roman theatrical drama. In Rome, as in Greece, it was rare for women to perform. Usually, both male and female roles were played by men, but for a particular type of comedy, called the *mimus*.

The *mimus* was a kind of lowbrow farce intended to depict the everyday lives and lecheries of the common folk. Adultery was a favorite subject and the language could be vulgar. Unlike other theatrical forms, the performers did not wear masks and attractive women were an integral part of the company, for it was not uncommon for these mimes to finish with the women taking off their clothes at an audience's urging. Although wildly popular with the masses, Roman intellectuals denounced this brand of entertainment, at least publicly. Tacitus lamented Rome's obsession with actors, gladiators, and horse racing, counting them among the vices that distracted the city's populace and kept them from pursuing loftier goals.[6]

Despite the negative social connotations, some actors, like their fellow performers in the arena, the gladiators, did achieve great wealth and fame, not to mention the adoration of the ladies. In addition to the tale of the smitten Eppia, Juvenal's diatribe against the faithlessness of upper-crust women contains several mentions of dalliances with actors. Actresses, however, seem to have been less able to transcend the bounds of class and status. The roles in which they were cast very often required that they expose themselves, a public display so dishonorable that their occupation became synonymous with prostitution. From the reign of the emperor Augustus, men of senatorial rank were forbidden to marry actresses. This law remained in place for five centuries, until Justinian, the future emperor of Byzantium, had it changed so he could wed the former actress Theodora.

From these depths of ignominy, *ludia* also came to refer to a woman in any way affiliated with a gladiatorial school, known as the *ludus*. Whether as groupie, paramour, or wife of a gladiator or as a combatant in her own right, the term seems to encompass a range of associations. The word appears twice in Juvenal's sixth satire, in which he decries the "Ways of Women." Scholars, however, are divided as to which meaning—or meanings—he intends. It is a problematic translation. In an early passage, he claims Eppia risks being mocked as a *ludia* by running off with a gladiator, and then later ridicules noble ladies who play at being gladiatrices for the ardor in which they train and the amount of heavy equipment they use, suggesting that no *ludia* would ever dress like that or fight so.[7] An epigram by Martial heaps great praise upon one Hermes, a gladiator named for a god. The most formidable of opponents, he was said to have been the cause of great distraction among the *ludiae*, proving both their darling and their dismay. The term here is taken to mean "gladiators' women," as this group would naturally be admiring of such an exceptional specimen of the games, but would also despair at the sight of him, fearing not for their own lives, but for those of their menfolk.[8]

Under certain circumstances, it seems, gladiators could and did legally marry. A tombstone to the gladiator Danaos, now in Vienna, was erected by his wife and son. In the relief, nine victory wreaths and weapons of the trade boast of the man's distinguished career, while the central scene provides an incongruous depiction of the deceased fighter in a tranquil domestic setting, surrounded by his wife, grown son, and family dog. The relationship between a couple in Britain is not as clear but no less intriguing. Their names and professions appear in a graffito found at Leicester, crudely scratched onto the surface of a small piece of broken pottery:

VERECUNDA LUDIA

LUCIUS GLADIATOR[9]

Was Verecunda an actress herself, traveling a separate path from her star-crossed lover, Lucius the gladiator? Was she simply a besotted fan, pining over her favorite in the troupe? Or was she something more to this man? Could she have been a gladiatrix herself? A hole pierced through the object suggests it was meant to be suspended on a thong and worn, perhaps as a magic charm or lover's remembrance. Which of the pair held it close to their heart, however, is unknown, as is their fate.

Juvenal paints a rather unflattering picture of women who chose to take up the sword:

Why need I tell of the purple wraps and the wrestling-oils used by women? Who has not seen one of them smiting a stump, piercing it through and through with a foil, lunging at it with a shield, and going through all the proper motions? A matron truly qualified to blow a trumpet at the Floralia![10] Unless, indeed, she is nursing some further ambition in her bosom, and is practicing for the real arena. What modesty can you expect in a woman who wears a helmet, abjures her own sex, and delights in feats of strength? Yet she would not choose to be a man, knowing the superior joys of womanhood. What a fine thing for a husband, at an auction of his wife's effects, to see her belt and armlets and plumes put up for sale, with a gaiter that covers half the left leg; or if she fights another sort of battle, how charmed you will be to see your young wife disposing of her greaves! Yet these are the women who find the thinnest of thin robes too hot for them; whose delicate flesh is chafed by the finest of silk tissue. See how she pants as she goes through her prescribed exercises; how she bends under the weight of her helmet; how big and coarse are the bandages which enclose her haunches; and then laugh when she lays down her arms and shows herself to be a woman![11]

Yet, despite the derision of the Roman intelligentsia, women of the higher orders seem to have flocked to the arena in such alarming numbers that the situation drew repeated official attention. In A.D. 19, a *senatus consultum* (senatorial decree) was passed prohibiting both men and women of the highest ranks from appearing on the stage or in the arena.[12] The document also makes reference to an earlier ruling from A.D. 11 that specifically forbade freeborn

women under the age of twenty from similarly demeaning themselves. Almost two centuries later, however, the ferocity with which
women still fought against each other in single combat so disturbed
the emperor Septimius Severus that, sometime around A.D. 200, he
extended the ban to include women of every station.[13]

Where these women could have learned their craft is a question
tackled by classicist Mark Vesley of the University of Minnesota.
He posits that the traditional gladiator schools were unfit for anything other than the dregs of society, certainly no place for thrill-
seeking aristocrats. They would have instead sought private
instruction or enrolled in *collegia iuvenum*, organized social clubs
where young men and women could pursue all manner of physical
activity, from gymnastics to martial arts. Among the evidence Vesley brings to bear is an inscription from Ostia, the port of Rome, in
which Hostilianus, a local magistrate, brags that he was "the first
since the city was founded . . . to set women fighting."[14] Presumably, this refers to the exhibition of female gladiators in the local
amphitheater, but Vesley finds it telling that this man was also
responsible for putting on the games of Ostia's *collegium iuvenum*.

Like their male counterparts, gladiatrices seem to have mastered
specialized forms of combat. Dio Cassius, writing of the reign of the
emperor Titus, mentions that *venatrices*, women skilled in fighting
wild beasts, participated in the dedication ceremonies for the inaugu-
ration of the Colosseum in A.D. 80.[15] Martial, too, makes reference to
these huntresses who put the labors of a demigod to shame:

Illustrious Fame used to sing of the lion laid low in Nemea's spa-
cious vale, Hercules' work. Let ancient testimony be silent, for

after your shows, Caesar, we have now seen such things done by women's valor.[16]

In Petronius' *Satyricon*, a guest at Trimalchio's feast speaks enthusiastically of an associate who is amassing his own gladiatorial troupe and already counts among his collection an *essedaria*, a gladiatrix who fought from a British-style war chariot.[17] It was this passage that inspired the scene in Ridley Scott's epic film *Gladiator*, in which the hero faces off against female gladiators astride speeding chariots in the Colosseum. Although there is little evidence to substantiate mixed-gender combat, Kathleen Coleman, the Harvard professor and classical scholar who served as historical advisor for the film, does believe the reference to *essedaria* hints at the possibility of woman gladiators from Britain:

> We know that there were chariot-borne gladiators, and in the novel by Petronius, which was written in the reign of Nero after Claudius had conquered Britain, there is a reference to, in a fictitious context obviously, a female chariot-borne gladiator. Now if the Romans, having encountered women driving chariots in Britain as we know they did, had transferred that to the familiar context of the arena, they might have come up with the idea of having a female gladiator on a chariot.

Julius Caesar, it seems, was particularly impressed by British chariots, mainstays of Celtic warfare. During his Gallic campaigns, Caesar made two Channel crossings with an eye toward invasion. He landed along the southeast coast of Britain, first with an expeditionary force in 55 B.C., then again the following year with a much larger complement. Although his ambitions were thwarted by foul weather and fierce resistance by local tribes, he did have opportunity to witness these vehicles of war in action:

> In chariot fighting the Britons begin by driving all over the field hurling javelins, and generally the terror inspired by the horses and the noise of the wheels are sufficient to throw their opponents' ranks into disorder. Then, after making their way between the squadrons of their own cavalry, they jump down from the chariots and engage on foot. In the meantime their charioteers retire a short distance from the battle and place the chariots in such a position that their masters, if hard-pressed by numbers, have an easy means of retreat to their own lines. Thus they combine the mobility of cavalry with the staying power of infantry; and by daily training and practice they attain such proficiency that even on a steep incline they are able to control the horses at full gallop, and to check and turn them in a moment. They can run along the chariot pole, stand on the yoke, and get back into the chariot as quick as lightning.[18]

Romans often brought their experiences in foreign lands into the amphitheater, constructing enormous set pieces re-creating famous battles or exotic locales in which tens, hundreds, and sometimes thousands of imported animals and prisoners of war would be sacrificed in the name of entertainment. In the grim world of the gladiators, however, performances were highly ritualized and steeped in symbolism, drawing upon both history and myth. This seems to have held true for the women as well as the men. In addition to the Statius poem in which gladiatrices were seen to evoke images of the Amazons, a relief from Halicarnassus also makes an association with these legendary warrior women.

Found on the west coast of Turkey in the nineteenth century, this relief, now housed in the British Museum, depicts two women locked in combat. It is one of the most solid pieces of evidence for the existence of women gladiators and has long fascinated scholars like Coleman:

> Two gladiators facing each other in a fighting stance, and they are heavily armed with these oblong curved shields. The left-hand gladiator is wearing an arm guard, which is composed of wrappings of leather around the length of the arm. She's also got a short sword, and so has the right-hand gladiator. Remarkably the breast is showing that this protagonist is clearly female. Unfortunately there is damage at breast height on the right-hand figure. The figure on the left has a very feminine hairstyle with a braid around the forehead and a bun at the nape of the neck. But the inscription at the bottom tells us incontrovertibly that these are both women because they are named Amazon and Achillia, the feminine form of the name Achilles, the name of one of the great Greek heroes. *Amazon* of course is the word for an Amazon in Greek.

Above their heads, a single word, *apelythesan*, is inscribed. This is a Greek term referring to their honorable retirement from the arena. In addition to the inscription, there are several clues in the depiction of these combatants that suggest they were formally trained gladiators competing for serious stakes. Coleman sees nothing "mocking" in their attire or "wimpish" in their stance. Unlike the aristocratic women Juvenal disparages, who simply played at being gladiators and could just as easily throw off their armor and return to their lives of luxury, the two women seen here are fighting for their freedom.

Although the largely male audience may well have been titillated at the sight of their bare torsos, the women's dress did not differ markedly from that of their male counterparts. They wear the costumes and bear the weapons traditionally associated with a type of gladiator known as a *provocator*. The only thing missing is their helmets, prompting Coleman to offer a new interpretation of the scene:

> There is one curious thing about them and that is that they are not wearing helmets. But there are two funny objects at the bottom on either side of the plinth that the figures are standing on and these rounded objects were once interpreted as spectators' heads, although it's rather a funny place for spectators to be positioned, relative to these combatants, and what I think we do have here are helmets.
>
> You can see the crown, the brim, the visor, and the neck guard, and these are presumably the helmets worn by the two women and they have taken them off. The question is: why? One of the things that signifies either the admission of defeat or at least the admission of having reached a stalemate is to remove one part of one's armor, either the shield or very commonly the helmet.
>
> You will notice that these helmets are resting right way up, they obviously have not fallen off, and they symbolize for the illiterate viewer the admission of a stalemate which generates the

result of a reprieve for both combatants. These women are being depicted as full-scale, proper paid-up gladiators.

They represented, as all gladiators did, the kernel quality of the arena which was *virtus*, which is courage, manly courage. The word *virtus* comes from the route *vir*, which means "man" in Latin, and the anomaly here of course is that this quality is being displayed by female combatants.

Achillia and Amazon were most likely stage names, but they grounded the women's performances in the well-known myths of the time. The nigh-invulnerable Greek hero, Achilles, and the fierce bands of warrior women, the Amazons, are both said to have fought in the Trojan War, but on opposing sides. Achilles is even attributed with killing one of the Amazons' leaders, Penthesilea.[19] She is described by Virgil in his *Aeneid*:

And battle-mad Penthesilea was there, leading the charge of Amazons carrying their crescent-shields; in the midst of thousands she blazed, showing her breast uncovered with a gold girdle clasped below, a warrior maid daring the shock of combat with men.[20]

Amazons appear in innumerable Greek and Roman tales and were an extremely popular motif in classical art. They are most often shown, in a kind of artistic shorthand, wearing a short dress, or chiton, that bares one breast. Traditionally, it was thought that the word "amazon" was derived from the Greek meaning "without breast," the rationale being that the surgical removal of the right breast would enable the women to be better shots with a bow. This seems to contradict most Greco-Roman portrayals, where both breasts are clearly intact, and more recent interpretations have taken the term to mean "those who are not breast-fed."[21]

Reliefs depicting an Amazonomachy, scenes of Greeks battling Amazons, graced the west side of the Parthenon in Athens. Ancient artists and authors alike were simultaneously fascinated and appalled by the notion of a society dominated by women:

> [W]ho could believe that an army of women, or a city, or a tribe, could ever be organized without men.[22]

Nomadic conquerors and nation-builders, their fame as peerless fighters led some to posit a divine lineage that traced back to the Greek god of war himself:

> [T]he Amazons were not gentle foes and regarded not justice, those dwellers on the Doeantian plain; but grievous insolence and the works of Ares were all their care; for by race they were the daughters of Ares and the nymph Harmonia, who bare to Ares war-loving maids.[23]

The fabled Amazonian capital, Themiscyra, was said to have been located along the southern Black Sea coast in what is now northern Turkey. This region fell under Roman control with the conquest of Asia Minor. With it may have come the legacy of these incomparable women, a legacy perhaps not as mythic as first supposed.

In the mid–fifth century B.C., the Greek writer Herodotus returned from his travels north of the Black Sea having heard stories of warrior women who rode the Russian steppes. According to him, their neighbors, the Scythians, called them *Oiorpata*, or "mankillers."

They were said to be descendants of the original Amazons who, having been driven from their homes on the southern shores of the Black Sea by the Greeks, journeyed north, mated with local men, and founded a new society on the grassy plains. Modern examinations of the corpus of Amazon myth have taken pains to dismiss such fantastic tales, preferring to interpret them as literary and ideological constructs—inverted mirrors of Greece's own male-dominated society—but recent archaeological discoveries in regions long closed to western scholarship are beginning to restore Herodotus's tarnished reputation as the "Father of History."

Following the fall of the Iron Curtain, Jeannine Davis-Kimball, director of the Center for the Study of Eurasian Nomads in Berkeley, California, was one of the first foreign investigators to work alongside archaeologists of the former Soviet Union to unravel the mystery of women warriors of the steppes. Her study of a cemetery site at Pokrovka, on the Russian border with Kazakhstan, included the excavation of fifteen burial mounds known as kurgans. Located in the southern sector of the cemetery complex, these kurgans contained numerous graves of both males and females dating from the Sauromatian and Sarmatian periods, spanning from the sixth century B.C. through the second century A.D.

Overall, the women's burials produced a much wider variety and greater quantity of artifacts than their male contemporaries found at the site. The most intriguing finds, however, came from seven graves of women and girls. These contained caches of weapons, including swords, daggers, arrowheads, and quivers. The skeletal remains of one girl, thirteen or fourteen years old, showed bowing in the legs that could have been the result of a life spent on horseback. She was laid to rest with an iron dagger and dozens of bronze arrowheads. In decades past, when Russian scholars encountered similarly outfitted women buried in kurgans, they were hesitant to say that these weapons accompanied the women in life as well as death, preferring to see them as purely ritual in purpose.

Tall in stature, strong and robust, the skeletons of some of the Pokrovka women also show signs of lives in harm's way. To Davis-Kimball this is evidence these women actively engaged in combat:

> We can definitely prove that the women were involved in warfare. We have excavated women that have had arrows actually embedded into bone and we have this female who suffered an extremely serious trauma, a blow on the head and then it has healed, causing this huge growth of bone.

As the Roman legions advanced eastward, the beliefs and stories of those they conquered made their way back to Rome. In addition to the legends of the Amazons, the Roman pantheon contained deities that came to be equated with Greek counterparts, including two well-known weapon-wielding goddesses: Minerva, identified with Athena, goddess of war and wisdom, and Diana, also known as Artemis, the goddess of the hunt. Minerva was the patroness of craftsmen and trade guilds, but also retained the martial aspects of her Greek parallel, invariably portrayed with helmet and spear. As Athena was the divine protector of the city of Athens, Minerva came to be included in the Capitoline Triad, the trio of deities officially worshipped throughout the empire as the supreme representatives of the Roman state.[24] Diana was a similarly multifaceted figure: In addition to ruling over the woodlands and all that dwelled within, she was a goddess of the moon and protector of women, particularly during childbirth.

The Romans had their own homegrown mythological heroines as well, among them, the mortal Camilla. Cast from a similar mold as the Amazons, she was a huntress and warrior favored by Diana. In Virgil's *Aeneid*, she leads a coed war band against the story's hero, Aeneas:

> [Camilla] was of Volscian race, and led her cavalcade of squadrons a-flower with bronze. She was a warrior; her girl's hands had never been trained to Minerva's distaff and her baskets of wool, but rather, though a maiden, she was one to face out grim fights and in speed of foot to outdistance the winds. She might have skimmed over the tops of uncut corn-stalks without ever harming their delicate ears as she ran, or upheld her way through the midst of the sea supported on the heaving waves without once wetting her swift-foot-soles in its surface. A gathering of mothers and all the young men who were streaming from houses and fields looked forth admiringly at her as she passed, in open-mouthed astonishment to see how regal splendour clothed her smooth shoulders in purple, how her brooch clasped her hair in its gold, and how she wore on her a Lycian quiver and carried a shepherd's myrtle-staff with a lance's head.[25]

Camilla's beginnings were equally remarkable. Her father, Metabus, driven from his city by a revolt, fled with his infant daughter. His enemies close at his heels, he came upon a river he could not possibly cross with little Camilla in his arms. Desperate and without options, Metabus tied the baby to a spear, and with a prayer consecrating the child's life to Diana, hurled it across the raging waters. When he struggled to the opposite shore, he was joyous to discover the spear with its precious cargo had also made it safely to the other side. The two went on to live in harmony among the shepherds in the woods, where Camilla remained faithful to the goddess who protected her, avoiding marriage and honing her skills with javelin, bow, and sling.[26]

The inhabitants of Britannia, however, did not need to look to distant myths from foreign lands for their inspiration. For them, the sight of a woman in battle would have held its own special meaning. Boudica, the Celtic queen of the Iceni, loomed large in their memories. In A.D. 60/61, she led her tribe and others in a revolt that nearly cost Rome the province.

In the years prior to its conquest, a succession of emperors had considered taking Britain as their prize. It was an attractive notion to follow in the footsteps of Julius Caesar and succeed where the great man had not. Taming the savage land and claiming it for Rome would do much to establish any emperor's authority, but nearly a century passed before the challenge was taken up in earnest.

In A.D. 43, the emperor Claudius mounted a full-scale invasion force and set off across the "Great Ocean" (the English Channel) at the behest of an ousted British chief who had fled to Rome for help. It was often Roman policy to nurture diplomatic ties with the tribal leaders situated along the frontiers of the empire. This strategy of providing gifts, loans, and even military assistance not only ensured a peaceful border, but also paved the way for the eventual annexation of these territories.

Only recently thrust into power following the assassination of his nephew, the reviled Caligula, Claudius was eager for an excuse to show off his prowess as a military commander and prove his worthiness to rule. The turmoil in Britain seemed tailor-made to suit his political needs, but it turned out to be no easy victory.

After meeting with some significant early successes, it was only a matter of days before Claudius hurried back to Rome to celebrate his triumph. The conquest was publicized throughout the empire. In a relief commemorating the event found at the site of Aphrodisias in southwest Turkey, Claudius, an older man, reputed to have suffered from some physical disability, is depicted in the guise of a well-muscled mythological hero standing victorious over a fallen Amazon meant to represent the vanquished Britannia. As he grasps the woman's hair with one hand, the other is poised to strike the final blow. Pinned beneath his knee, Britannia writhes and raises a hand in a plea for mercy. The irony of such a scene would be left to the following generation, when a British queen stood against the might of Rome and taught its people some hard lessons they would not soon forget.

The Roman strategy of supporting allied nations along the empire's fringes, which had worked so well in the past, would come back to haunt them in Britain. Mounting gifts and loans extended to the local aristocratic families had left them indebted and in debt to Rome. The situation strained relations with supposedly "friendly" tribes that had been allowed to remain nominally independent, while the Roman administration concentrated on quelling hostile rebels in the west and uprisings in the north.

This ever-shifting political landscape hampered efforts to expand the fledgling province, but did not stop the founding of several Roman towns and colonies. Populated by retired army veterans, sympathetic Britons, and foreign merchants, these urban centers quickly thrived and grew. In doing so, however, the immigrant population may have overstepped themselves and contributed to the mounting ill will among the locals.

The flashpoint finally came when Prasutagus, king of the Iceni, passed away in A.D. 60 or 61.[27] He had reigned in what is now East Anglia as an ally and client of Rome, but upon his death, in accordance with Roman policy, all existing treaties became null and void. Hoping to protect his kingdom and retain at least some autonomy for his descendants, Prasutagus had named his two young daughters as heirs jointly with Nero, who had by then succeeded Claudius as emperor. This unconventional arrangement went unrecognized by Rome, and the Iceni lands and people were now expected to be subsumed into the province and fall under direct Roman governance.

These expectations were acted upon with alarming speed and brutality. Shortly after the king's death, representatives of the province's chief financial officer, the procurator Catus Decianus, were dispatched and forcibly began to strip Iceni nobles of their property and hereditary estates.

The historian Tacitus recalls the objections of the besieged populace:

> The governor has centurions to execute his will; the procurator, slaves; and both of them add insults to violence. Nothing is any longer safe from their greed and lust. In war it is at least a braver man who takes the spoil; as things stand with us, it is mostly cowards and shirkers that seize our homes, kidnap our children, and conscript our men.[28]

The greatest abuses and humiliation, however, were visited upon the king's own family. His daughters were raped and Boudica, his widow, was flogged. This was more than the people could stand and they rose in revolt, led by the queen herself.

Boudica, her very name derived from the Celtic word for "victory," made a lasting impression on the Roman psyche.[29] Even a century and a half later, when described by another historian, Dio Cassius, she is an imposing figure:

> In stature she was very tall, in appearance most terrifying, in the glance of her eye most fierce, and her voice was harsh; a great mass of the tawniest hair fell to her hips; around her neck was a large golden necklace; and she wore a tunic of divers colors over which a thick mantle was fastened with a brooch. This was her invariable attire. She now grasped a spear to aid her in terrifying all beholders.[30]

Tacitus and Dio are our only authorities on the revolt of A.D. 60/61, but both place Boudica as its driving force:

> [T]he person who was chiefly instrumental in rousing the natives and persuading them to fight the Romans, the person who was thought worthy to be their leader and who directed the conduct of the entire war, was Boudica, a Briton woman of the royal family and possessed of greater intelligence than often belongs to women.[31]
>
> . . . [T]he whole island rose under the leadership of Boudica, a lady of royal descent—for Britons make no distinction of sex in their appointments of commanders.[32]

Her revenge was swift and terrible, catching the Roman forces off guard. Not expecting trouble from an area thought long subdued, the provincial governor, C. Suetonius Paulinus, was off on a military campaign in north Wales. He was in the process of mounting an assault on the Druid sanctuary on the island of Mona (modern Anglesey) when he got word of the uprising.

What was thought to be a populace already cowed and bent to the Roman yoke turned out to have been harboring years of frustration and pent-up resentment just waiting to boil over. The Iceni's neighbors, the Trinovantes, quickly joined their cause. Their traditional seat of power, Camulodunum (modern Colchester), had been personally captured by Claudius in the early days of the invasion. Soon after, a Roman colony was established at that location, smugly dubbed *Colonia Victricensis* ("City of Victory"), and settled with army veterans. These former soldiers were purported to have treated the native population abominably. Adding insult to injury, a triumphal arch commemorating the conquest was erected in the town. This monument may have been the twin of one at Rome whose inscription boasts of the surrender of eleven British kings and lauds Claudius as the first to bring the barbarians under Roman control.[33] Intended to serve as the capital of the new province, Camulodunum also became the local seat of the imperial cult, with a temple dedicated to the divine Claudius. For all these reasons and more, Camulodunum became the first target for the tribes' fury.

Terrible portents were said to have foretold of the coming storm:

[F]or no visible reason, the statue of Victory at Camulodunum fell down—with its back turned as though it were fleeing the enemy.

Delirious women chanted of destruction at hand. They cried that in the local senate-house outlandish yells had been heard; the theater had echoed with shrieks; at the mouth of the Thames a phantom settlement had been seen in ruins. A blood-red color in the sea, too, and shapes like human corpses left by the ebb tide, were interpreted hopefully by the Britons—and with terror by the settlers.[34]

The colonists at Camulodunum caught wind of the impending attack. With the provincial governor still detained with the affairs at Mona on the other side of the island, they appealed to Catus Decianus for assistance, but the callous procurator was only able to spare a couple hundred inadequately armed men. The town itself was poorly fortified, so the settlers hoped to make their stand from within the precinct walls of the temple of Claudius. Tacitus reports that secret Boudican sympathizers among the populace hampered efforts to build additional defenses, nor were women and the elderly evacuated to safety.

A detachment from the ninth legion rushed from their garrison in the Midlands to rescue the town, but were ambushed en route. The entire force of infantry, some fifteen hundred troops, was annihilated and the cavalry put to rout. After two days under siege, the temple barricades were overrun. The whole of Camulodunum was put to the torch and its population slaughtered.

While Procurator Catus Decianus beat a hasty retreat back to the European mainland, Governor Suetonius Paulinus headed for London, the next town in the path of Boudica's merciless army. As with Camulodunum, the burgeoning commercial center was lacking in sufficient fortifications. After quickly assessing the lay of the land, Suetonius made the difficult tactical decision to abandon the place to its fate in order to take up a more defensible position elsewhere. The inhabitants of London, mainly merchants and immigrant craftsmen, were beside themselves, and begged the governor to reconsider, but Suetonius would not be swayed. He marched on, taking with him all the able-bodied men of London who opted to join the fight and leaving the women, children, old, and infirm behind to be massacred. Once again, the city was set alight.

The town of Verulamium, populated by Romanized Britons of the Catuvellauni tribe, was the next to fall to Boudica's wrath, and along the way, several more isolated homes and farmsteads were destroyed. Tacitus describes the bloody swathe cut through the countryside:

> The natives enjoyed plundering and thought of nothing else. Bypassing forts and garrisons, they made for where loot was richest and protection weakest. Roman and provincial deaths at the places mentioned are estimated at seventy thousand. For the British did not take or sell prisoners, or practice other war-time exchanges. They could not wait to cut throats, hang, burn, and crucify—as though avenging, in advance, the retribution that was on its way.[35]

Dio, for his part, recounts particular depravities in lurid detail:

> The worst and most bestial atrocity committed by their captors was the following. They hung up naked the noblest and most distinguished women and then cut off their breasts and sewed them to their mouths, in order to make the victims appear to be eating them; afterwards they impaled the women on sharp skewers run lengthwise through the entire body.[36]

Despite the terrible toll exacted upon soldiers and civilians alike, Roman writers treat Boudica herself with considerable respect, depicting her as a powerful, independent noblewoman motivated by fierce pride to avenge her personal honor and that of her people. Tacitus imagines the eloquent speech with which she rallied her troops before the final climactic battle:

> Boudica drove round all the tribes in a chariot with her daughters in front of her. "We British are used to women commanders in war," she cried. "I am descended from mighty men! But now I am not fighting for my kingdom and wealth. I am fighting as an ordinary person for my lost freedom, my bruised body, and my outraged daughters. Nowadays Roman rapacity does not even spare our bodies. Old people are killed, virgins raped. But the gods will grant us the vengeance we deserve! The Roman division which dared to fight is annihilated. The others cower in their camps, or watch for a chance to escape. They will never face even the din and roar of our thousands, much less the shock of our onslaught. Consider how many of you are fighting—and why. Then you will win this battle, or perish. That is what I, a woman, plan to do! Let the men live in slavery if they will."[37]

But her brave words were not enough. Suetonius, arriving in advance of Boudica's army, chose the battlefield and took the strategic high ground. The British forces had to advance along a narrow pass, with wagons bearing their families and possessions in tow. Although numerically superior, they were unable to hold out against the discipline and tactics of the Roman military. In their retreat, they became hopelessly entangled among the heavily laden wagons and dying pack animals to their rear. Tacitus estimates nearly eighty thousand Britons died that day.

Rather than face further humiliation at Roman hands, Boudica took poison and died. Tacitus is mute as to what happened next, but Dio claims her body was spirited away by her compatriots and given a costly burial as befitted a revered leader.

> [A]ll this ruin was brought upon the Romans by a woman, a fact which in itself caused them the greatest shame.[38]

Boudica's rampage across southeastern England left tens of thousands dead and three cities in ruins, among them London. Ten years later, a new city had been built atop the remains of the old. With it came the amphitheater where the appearance of women in the arena would have served as a double-edged reminder of the province's hard-won history, of the dangers of Roman complacency, and the price of resistance.

Camilla's sword bit deep into the thick hide covering Myrine's shield, lodging in the wood beneath. Once again, Myrine was quick to take advantage of her opponent's momentary vulnerability. Exposed and off balance, Camilla barely had time to wrench her weapon free and deflect Myrine's uppercut.

Safely behind the curve of her own large shield, Camilla looked at her adversary with new eyes. She was not as green as first thought: She gave as good as she got. Someone had trained her well. And, in underestimating the young fighter, Camilla was almost drawn into making a rookie mistake herself.

They were evenly matched, each with short swords. Anything that extended beyond their heavy shields—arms, legs, head—was protected by armor. This leant itself to subtle, close-quarters fighting. Subtle did not play well to the cheap seats, however.

Camilla shoved Myrine away and took several steps back. "Come at me," she urged.

"What?"

"Come at me. Show your friends up in the women's section what you can do."

"I have no friends there!" Myrine screamed and lunged at Camilla.

Bitter and a fast study, thought Camilla. *I'm beginning to like this girl.*

A furious exchange of overly dramatic, crowd-pleasing blows ensued, but Camilla could tell by the reaction from the stands that they were not the center of attention.

She glanced over just in time to see Heraklia forced to her knees as she struggled with Agave. Agave played her part of the frenzied Bacchant to the hilt. What was supposed to be her thyrsus, the festive willow wand carried by the followers of the god Bacchus, was in reality a long-handled cudgel with a nasty iron spike embedded in its head, with which she flailed away with wild abandon. Heraklia was on the defensive and looking pretty desperate—her own weapon lay on the ground, well out of reach.

Why hadn't the referees suspended the fight so Heraklia could retrieve her blade? The sound of the crowd answered her question: They wanted blood.

But they weren't to get Heraklia's blood, Camilla decided. Not today.

With a shout, Camilla threw her sword to her friend. The spectators gasped as one. The referees were livid, but unsure how to punish such a blatant infraction of the rules: Stop the fight or let it continue? The cheer that went up when Heraklia caught the weapon made their decision for them.

"What are you doing?!" cried Myrine, as she hacked frantically at Camilla's shield. "You're going to get us both killed!"

Camilla withstood the battery, slowly edging back to where she saw

Heraklia's sword lying in the dust. But when she reached the spot, a vindictive referee kicked it away. Now what?

The audience let out a tremendous roar, reassuring her that Heraklia had managed to dispatch Agave. At least one of them had the gods on her side this day.

Myrine caught her in a clinch. "Now's our chance," she whispered. "Take off your helmet."

This possibility hadn't even occurred to Camilla. "I can't!"

"You have to. It's the only way. I can't go on much longer—my arm's like wet wool. If we both do it, they might show us mercy."

It was a long shot, but Camilla reluctantly agreed. It'd been ten long, hard years—what were the odds he would recognize her? Together, they threw down their helmets and turned to the sponsor's box to meet their fate.

Ten years, apparently, were not long enough. As her father rose to deliver his verdict, his gaze fixed on Camilla. She read his mind on his face: first puzzlement, then shock, and then dread. There, standing before him, covered in the dust, sweat, and blood of the arena, was his daughter come back to haunt him.

❧ 3 ❧

ROMAN WOMEN: *VIRGO, MATRONA, LUPA*

Ever class-conscious, Romans turned their backs on status and reputation at their own risk. To rise too far above one's station or stoop below it was an invitation to criticism and scorn. Juvenal vilifies the blue-blooded Eppia not simply because she had abandoned her role as the traditional Roman wife and mother when she left husband, family, and hearth behind, but because she had done so to take up with a lowly, used-up gladiator. What would have prompted a woman of her stature to cast off her privileged existence to follow her heart? What was to be gained in chancing the uncertainties of life on society's fringes?

Juvenal's views may have been exaggerated for the sake of satire, but by reading between the vitriol, it is possible to get a sense of the expectations placed on women's behavior. Eppia is just one of numerous examples Juvenal marshals to illustrate the perils of women who too easily forget their place. He condemns the ways of "modern" women as lascivious, faithless, greedy, and headstrong where they should be chaste, pious, reserved, and dutiful. Independence is more vice than virtue. In the Roman world, a woman's life was rarely her own, coming under the control of first her father and then her husband. Her opportunities were constrained by the rigid bounds of society and propriety.

Roman society was one of social divisions. Foremost was the distinction between insider and outsider, citizen and foreigner. As the empire grew to encompass more diverse territories and peoples, citizenship was meted out as an honor and a privilege. It was an exclusive membership, affording provincials the right of legal recourse under Roman law and the ability to participate in their own governance, as well as opportunities for financial and political advancement within the Roman system. By the end of the first century A.D., it was even possible for someone like Trajan, who hailed from the Roman province of Hispania Baetica in southern Spain, to ascend to the highest office of emperor.

Trajan's origins, however, were hardly humble. Coming from an old, established Italian family with a long history of political and military service to the empire, he owed his ascension to family connections and his own distinguished career. His father had held governorships in Spain, Syria, and Asia, while Trajan himself was governor of Upper Germany when he was appointed heir to the emperor Nerva. To be born a citizen was certainly more prestigious than having it bestowed upon you, but to Romans, the family into which you were born made all the difference.

Within the Roman social structure, there were two citizen classes: patricians and plebeians. The patricians were society's elite, a small group of wealthy landowning families who wielded a dispro-portionate amount of power and influence. A hereditary aristocracy with its origins in Rome's early history, all major political and reli-gious officials were initially appointed from these few leading fami-lies. Intermarriage with plebeians, who constituted the general citizenry, was long prohibited, effectively barring them from power. Patricians were the priests, the senators and consuls, and, later, the emperors.

From the fifth century B.C. onward, however, the plebes fought to loosen the patrician's stranglehold. After two centuries of strug-gle, they succeeded in securing greater representation for them-selves, including their own assemblies and magistracies, as well as gaining access to the Senate. The interdiction against marriage between the two classes was also lifted. Over the years, the fortunes of individual patrician and plebeian families rose and fell. Distinc-tions became blurred as some plebes successfully exploited the new commercial opportunities that arose with Roman expansion, oppor-tunities that competed with the traditional agrarian-based economy of the patricians. The pathways to power, however, were still paved with gold and remained in the hands of the wealthiest few.

A large—and largely unsung—segment of Roman society was the enslaved. There are estimates that, by the end of the republican period, one quarter to nearly a third of the entire population of the city of Rome were slaves. Captured in war, the spoils of conquest, or obtained through trade, slaves were an integral part of Roman life. A Roman of even modest means might hope to own one or two while, at the other end of the spectrum, the more affluent might have dozens, even hundreds, to tend to their villas, manufacturing industries, and vast agricultural estates. Slaves filled a variety of niches, from unskilled farm laborers to domestic servants to craftsmen to personal secretaries.

Slaves had no rights. They were the property of their masters to do with as they willed. As possessions, they could be punished or disposed of, sold or even executed if they transgressed. They could not legally marry and any children born to a slave automatically became the property of the master. Conditions could be harsh and treatment cruel, as evidenced by several mass slave revolts, including that of gladiators led by Spartacus from 73 to 71 B.C.

Conversely, maintaining a slave could be costly and needed to be seen as good value for the investment. Slaves with special skills or particular intelligence were especially prized. As with using one's body, working with one's hands was an unsavory way for a respectable Roman to make a living. Artisans and craft workers, even physicians, architects, and teachers, often began their careers as gifted slaves.

Slaves whose talents and devotion pleased or brought profit to their owners were sometimes rewarded with manumission, either during their master's lifetime by formal decree or posthumously in their wills. These freed men and women probably represented a very small, but highly visible, minority. As former slaves, they lacked some of the basic rights of freeborn citizens, yet the same aptitudes—be they education, artistic skills, or business acumen—that gained them their eventual emancipation also occasionally propelled them to great prosperity. In particular, imperial slaves who had served as clerks or secretaries, minor government functionaries, or even advisors to the emperor himself, continued to enjoy positions of power and influence after being granted their freedom.

While some freedmen could afford to live in considerable luxury, they were regarded as the ultimate in nouveau riche, never truly accepted by their "betters" despite every attempt to imitate them in style and manner. This social ambivalence is played to great effect in Petronius' *Satyricon*, where the freed slave Trimalchio and his wife throw a banquet full of crass excess and outrageous behavior.

The fundamental building block of Roman society was the family, or *familia*. In an age when state- or community-sponsored social welfare was inconsistent at best, kin associations provided a necessary support network for the individual. The family was the hedge against old age, infirmity, and impoverishment. Romans traced their lineage through the males, and the family consisted of all descendants of the same father (*pater*). The definition of *familia*, however, often encompassed more than just blood relations: It could include the slaves of the household, freed former slaves, and even unrelated freeborn dependents (such as the descendants of the family's freedmen). Every individual, in turn, was responsible to their family and had to abide by the decisions of the *paterfamilias*, the oldest living progenitor of the line.

The power of the *paterfamilias* over his dependents was absolute. Even after children had grown and were living under a different roof, they were still beholden to him. It was not until a father's death that a son could come into his own and become a *paterfamilias* himself, although it was possible for an adult son to seek official emancipation while his father was still living. Authority over a daughter, however, was not so easily dissolved. Prior to the late first century B.C., it could only be transferred, either to a husband at marriage or to a male relation, or *tutor*, upon the death of the father.

The *paterfamilias* had a say in the lives of his sons' children, though not those of any daughters, as they would be born into their own fathers' *familia*. Slaves and their offspring remained in the possession of the *paterfamilias* unless sold to another. If granted their freedom, they would adopt their master's name, further cementing their association with the *familia*. Descendents of these freed slaves, themselves freeborn, would continue to look to the former owner's family for patronage and would honor that family's ancestral gods.

In addition to controlling all the financial assets of the family, the *paterfamilias'* legal rights (the *patria potestas*) gave him the authority to act in the interests of the family in what would today be considered more personal matters. He arranged marriages for his children and wards, and could order their divorce if a union proved no longer advantageous, regardless of the couple's feelings for each other. His power was so total that he could disown his own children if he disapproved of their behavior or sell them into slavery. He could even judge them privately and sentence them to death if he found their actions warranted it, as it was his responsibility to protect the family name and uphold its honor. Conversely, he was also obligated to protect and promote his dependents and could be held accountable for their actions.

Although the rights of the *paterfamilias* were vast, custom—if not a father's love and concern—constrained his actions. There are only a few examples of a father serving as the ultimate moral arbiter, most of these coming from the legendary days of Rome's early history. Such was the tragic tale of Verginia who, in the mid–fifth century B.C., became the pawn in a love triangle. Appius Claudius, a powerful commissioner, hatched a plot to break the maiden's engagement to another so he could have her for himself. He enlisted a crony to claim she was the man's slave and not a freeborn woman as she pretended. Appius Claudius himself presided over Verginia's trial, thinking that he would come to possess her in her disgrace; however, Verginia's noble father, distraught over the false verdict, took up a knife and killed her, as it was the only way he could see to protect the unfortunate girl's honor.[1]

In this man's world, a woman's life was highly circumscribed. Expectations were that she would marry, bear children, and manage her husband's household. These were the sole duties of a proper wife and girls were groomed for this role from an early age. Although a patriarchal culture, the Roman emphasis on family and succession did mean that women were an important part of this equation. The crowning glory of a woman's achievement was the production of healthy heirs to carry on her husband's name.

Pregnancy, however, was an extremely risky undertaking and many women died as a result. There was considerable pressure to start a family quickly after marriage, despite the fact that many girls wed barely into their teens, practically children themselves. Miscarriage, too, seems to have been a tragically frequent occurrence. High infant mortality rates during the Roman period meant that a woman had to face the dangers of childbirth time and again in order to ensure a few of her children survived into adulthood. That paragon of motherhood, Cornelia, the noble daughter, wife, and mother of famous men of the Roman Republic, was known as the "Mother of the Gracchi," but of the twelve children she bore, only three lived to carry on the family's illustrious reputation.

For those who wished to avoid pregnancy, methods of contraception were well-known in the ancient world, as were the means to induce abortion, but Romans considered these to be contradictory to the very purpose of marriage, which was procreation. Such techniques were probably most in demand in the case of extramarital affairs, prostitution, or liaisons with slaves. Any children produced from relations outside of wedlock were illegitimate and took their mother's name.[2] They had no claim to their biological father's household or legacy unless legally adopted by him.

The physician Soranus wrote at length on women's reproductive issues at the end of the first century A.D. He prefaces his remarks on preventatives by raising the age-old controversy over abortion among health practitioners. Some opposed the procedures on principle, as they were contrary to Hippocratic teachings, while others only advocated their use when a mother's welfare was in jeopardy. For his part, Soranus considered contraception preferable to the risks to the woman inherent in abortion but goes on to outline the favored techniques for both.[3]

Birth control was not only the last resort of those on the periphery of society or the impoverished who could not afford another mouth to feed; affluent families, too, might choose to curb the size of the generation due to inherit in order to preserve the family fortune by dividing it between fewer heirs. The dwindling size of families was such a cause for concern for the emperor Augustus that he drafted a series of legislation to urge couples to have more children.

Roman women gave birth at home, out of the sight of men, but this was by no means a small, private event. An expectant mother would be attended by the women of the household and one or more midwives.[4] If a pregnant woman was widowed or divorced before giving birth, representatives of the absent father's family would also bear witness on the day to confirm the newborn's legitimacy as heir to their line. Apparently, this custom could generate quite a crowd as, by the end of the first century B.C., it was necessary to pass a law limiting the size of the former in-laws' delegation to no more than ten women of free status, two midwives, and six female slaves.[5]

A small terra-cotta relief from a woman's tomb from Ostia bears a rare depiction of a childbirth scene. A woman in labor sits upright, clutching at the armrests of a specially designed birthing chair. Another woman supports her from behind, arms wrapped around the mother-to-be's chest. The midwife stoops before them on a low stool, preparing to deliver the baby.

After birth, a midwife would swaddle the baby and place it on the ground to be taken up and officially recognized by the *paterfamilias*. It was the father's prerogative to accept a newborn into his household or reject it. If a baby was unwanted for any reason, whether sick or deformed, or if the family was unable (or unwilling, particularly if illegitimate) to provide for it, the infant could be killed by suffocation or left exposed to the elements in some public location, where it would either expire or be picked up by a passing stranger and raised as a slave.

There are indications that baby girls were more often exposed than boys.[6] Girls may have been viewed as a greater financial burden. Hindered by their gender from seeking work outside the home to support the family, they also required the provision of dowries for marriage. Early Roman law, traditionally attributed to Romulus, the city's legendary founder, called for citizens to rear every male child but only the firstborn among the females. Evidence that this custom was put into practice comes from a letter dating to 1 B.C. from Oxyrhynchus, Egypt. In it, a husband away on business in Alexandria instructs his pregnant wife that if she gives birth during his absence, to let the child live if it is a boy, but to expose it if it is a girl.[7]

For many others, however, the birth of a healthy baby was a

welcomed and joyous occasion, whatever the sex. Infant mortality was extremely high, with estimates that half of all children born did not live to see their tenth birthday, most of these dying in their very first year. Despite these terrible odds, a successful birth was cause for celebration. In Pompeii, several birth announcements have been found scrawled across exterior house walls, one happily proclaiming the arrival of a baby girl.[8]

On a girl child's eighth day of life, she officially received her name (for boys, this occurred on their ninth) in a naming ceremony called the *dies lustricus*.[9] Romans of the upper classes followed a tripartite naming scheme for males (*tria nomina*), consisting of the *praenomen*, *nomen*, and *cognomen*. The *praenomen* was selected from a limited number of familiar names (Marcus, Lucius, Gaius, and the like) for use within the family and among intimates. The *nomen* was the hereditary name of the line, or *gens*, while the *cognomen* was often derived from a nickname or personal honor awarded an individual, which was later passed down to his descendants and served to identify a specific branch of a family.[10]

For females, however, naming conventions were much simpler, using only the feminized form of the *nomen* (and perhaps an inherited *cognomen*, just for good measure). Thus, Gaius Julius Caesar's daughter, sister, and paternal aunt were all named Julia, after the Julian clan, or *gens Julia*. Birth order was often employed to distinguish between identically named women within the same family, appending to the end of the name "older" (*maior*) or "younger" (*minor*), "first" (*prima*), "second" (*secunda*), "third" (*tertia*), and so on.

Slave names did not reflect parentage, having been bestowed upon them by slave traders or their masters upon birth or purchase. Often, they were called by a single Greek-sounding name, even if they themselves were not Greek.[11] Upon manumission, a freed male slave would take his master's *praenomen* and *nomen*, appending the name they were known by as a slave to the end as a *cognomen*, while a freedwoman might only adopt a feminized form of the *nomen*.

Not long after birth, it was customary for those who could to hand an infant over to a wet nurse, usually a slave or freedwoman attached to the household for this specific purpose. It may have been considered overly burdensome for a proper Roman matron to nurse her own children, but the image of a child suckling at its mother's breast remained a pervasive symbol of fertility, especially in areas where pre-Roman mother goddesses, the *Matres* or *Matronae*, continued to hold sway even after Roman conquest. Small pipe-clay statuettes, perhaps votive figures, have been found throughout the western provinces, depicting a woman seated in a high-backed wicker chair with one or two babies at her breast. In a relief in the Marburg Museum, a woman and child can be seen bringing offerings to this goddess, who is also sometimes identified as the *Dea Nutrix*. In a mid–second century funerary relief in the Louvre, a woman of privilege is shown nursing a child as a testament to her motherly concern for the child's welfare. Whether she breast-fed her own children in life, however, is unknown, but some took it as a point of pride. On a tombstone from Rome, a husband takes care to mention that his deceased wife "brought up her children with the milk of her own breasts."[12]

Regardless of which side of the breast-feeding debate a Roman family came down on, nurses continued to play an important role in children's lives for several years, often until puberty and beyond. They saw to the physical, social, and educational needs of their small charges along with the pedagogue, usually a male slave who also served as escort and protector when the child reached school age and ventured more frequently out into the world. Their child's constant companions, parents were advised to take particular care when contracting for nurses and other child minders. Bonds formed between guardian and child during these formative years often lasted into adulthood. It was said that upon a child's death, "the grief of a nurse comes next to that of a mother."[13] Pliny the Younger's affection for his old nurse is apparent in his gift of a small farm from which he ensured she would be able to draw an income in her later years.[14]

Given the fragility of life, particularly among the very young, the practice of exposure at birth and the employment of long-term caregivers, some scholars have questioned to what degree Romans allowed themselves to become emotionally attached to their children.[15] From the lengths many went to protect children from harm and disease with apotropaic amulets and rites, there is definitely evidence for abiding parental concern. The *bulla*, for example, was a charm given to a child at their naming ceremony. A pouch-shaped locket made of leather or, if the family could afford it, gold, it was intended to ward off malicious spirits and protect the wearer from the evil eye throughout their childhood. Removing it was a gesture signifying an individual's passage into adulthood. Boys took off their *bulla* when they received their toga of manhood and girls removed theirs on the day of their wedding.

The moving sentiments expressed on a tombstone from Ostia seem unequivocal:

My baby Acerva was snatched away to live in Hades before she had had her fill of the sweet light of life. She was beautiful and charming, a little darling as if from heaven. Her father weeps for her, and because he is her father asks that the earth may rest lightly on her forever.[16]

There appears little room to doubt this couple's inconsolable grief over the loss of their daughter, until compared with other, similarly eloquent epitaphs. Many lament lives of beauty and promise cut short and request that the earth not lie heavily upon the deceased. The language of such inscriptions tended to follow a prescribed formula, making it difficult to gauge the depth of feeling behind them.

A more personal testament can be found, perhaps, in the funerary statues of young girls. These touchingly rendered memorials were carved as busts or as full-length sculptures, in the round or as part of a tomb relief. Many were intended to be true likenesses, attempts to capture the individuality and personality of loved ones lost. In these portraits, girls are often shown accompanied by their favorite toys and pets, just as actual cherished playthings, such as dolls and pull-toys, were sometimes included in children's burials.

In writing to Aefulanus Marcellinus to inform him of the death of the daughter of a mutual friend, Pliny the Younger advises that he avoid "conventional expressions of consolation" when communicating with the despondent father but rather be "soft and sympathetic" so fresh is his grief.[17] Pliny remembers the girl, Minicia Marcella, fondly:

I've never seen anyone more cheerful or agreeable or worthy of a long life—even immortality—than that girl. She was just under fourteen but was as wise as an old woman and as sedate as a matron without losing her girlish sweet and virginal modesty. How she would throw her arms around her father's neck! How she loved her nurses and pedagogues and teachers for the services they provided her! How studiously and intelligently she read, and how sparingly she played! She suffered her last illness with such sobriety, patience, and constancy. She did as she was told by the doctors, and she cheered up her sister and father. When her body could no longer support her, her spirit went on till the last, broken neither by the illness itself nor fear of death.[18]

Pliny considers Minicia's passing to be all the more tragic as she was soon to be married. Childhood was brief for Roman girls and Minicia, although hardly a teenager,[19] was already seen to embody many of the virtues of womanhood. She was wise and mature, demure and obedient, serious, with an exceptional fortitude of spirit. She was on the very brink of achieving that which all Roman women should aspire: to become a wife and mother.

By age twelve, any formal education a girl might receive outside the home was ended and her time was devoted to household tasks befitting a woman of her station.[20] Education beyond what was necessary to supervise a household was not a high priority for women. A more learned husband might make an effort to supplement his wife's basic education so that she could better appreciate the work that he did. Such was the case with Pliny the Younger and his third wife, Calpurnia, whom he married when he was in his forties and she was decades his junior. In a letter, Pliny happily remarks on the girl's eagerness to read literature and memorize his own writings, seeing her interest as a reflection of her affection for him.[21] Juvenal, however, derided women who flaunted their knowledge or openly expressed opinions on subjects such as history, philosophy, or politics.[22]

Instead, wool-working seems to have been a particularly commendable pastime for women, for which they received special mention in their eulogies. This was not necessarily because they were weavers or spinners of any exceptional note, but rather it was intended to signify their adherence to traditional values, choosing to stay at home and fill their hours with the tedium of housework instead of in pursuit of less savory diversions, like attending the theater or the games. In the past, Juvenal claims, before Rome's prosperity opened the floodgates to idleness and promiscuity, a virtuous woman could be known for her hard work, lack of sleep, and gnarled hands from carding fleece.[23]

Roman women led nothing like the sequestered lives of their counterparts in ancient Greece, but they were still expected to limit their energies to the domestic sphere. Sempronia, an upper-class Roman matron, scandalized all by taking active part in the intrigues of the Catilinarian Conspiracy of 63 B.C. In addition to her participation in the exclusively male realm of politics, the historian Sallust counts among her many character flaws the ability to "play the lyre and dance . . . with more skill than is necessary for an honest woman."[24]

The eulogy of a woman called Murdia delivered by her son in Rome in the late first century B.C. illustrates just how narrow a woman's opportunities were seen to have been. He honors her for the loyalty, obedience, and good sense she showed in her marriages arranged by her parents, and for the just way in which she divided her estate in her will. After that, he seems at a loss for how to distinguish his mother's achievements from any others, stating that "in lives tossed by smaller storms there is less room for original ways to praise women" and that she was "like other good women in her modesty, decency, chastity, obedience, wool-work, zeal, and loyalty."[25]

Girls married young and there was often a considerable discrepancy in the ages of husband and wife. It was not uncommon for girls to wed by the age of twelve or thirteen and to be betrothed well before. With few exceptions, most women were married by their early twenties.[26] Men tended to marry later, in their mid-twenties or early thirties.

Marriages were arranged to benefit the families involved, seen as political, social, and economic alliances. The intent was to improve the wealth and position of both families. At the betrothal ceremony, the two families met to exchange gifts and finalize details, such as the dowry, then signed a formal agreement or announced their intentions before witnesses. The engagement was then sealed with a kiss between the betrothed and afterward friends and relatives came together to celebrate the happy occasion.

On the appointed day, the bridegroom led a procession to his fiancée's house where he was met by his bride. She would be dressed in a long white tunic, while her veil and shoes were orange or similarly flame-colored. Her gown, the *tunica recta*, was belted with a woolen girdle, tied in a specific manner meant to ward off evil. Her hair, too, was done up in a symbolic coiffure, parted using the tip of a bent iron spear. Although the meaning behind the act is not clear, it is known that a spearhead used to kill a gladiator was considered particularly potent magic in this instance.[27] By time her groom arrived, she had already prepared to leave the home of her birth through a series of rituals in which she gave up her childhood attire, including her *bulla*, and dedicated her toys to the household gods. After the marriage contract was signed, the rest of the day was taken up by feasting and ceremony, including a custom in which the groom and his party ritually seized the bride from her mother's arms.[28] Afterward, there would be a boisterous torchlit procession to the groom's residence, with attendants bearing the woman's most important tools, her spindle and distaff, to her new home. Once there, the husband would carry his new wife over the threshold, lest she trip (a bad omen for their future together).

There were two possible types of unions: In one, the woman and her property was transferred into the control (*manus*) of her husband, and in the other, the woman remained under the authority of her father. If a woman married *cum manu*, she became a part of her new husband's family and severed all ties with her own. She gave up her position in her father's familia and her right of inheritance through that line. Although this was the most common arrangement in Rome's early history, by the end of the Republic, it had all but fallen out of vogue. Families preferred to retain their close bonds to their daughters and, with them, their dowries, should the marriage come to an end through death or divorce.

Intended to provide solely for her maintenance, a woman's dowry could also be an important source of capital for a fledgling household. The *paterfamilias* controlled the wealth and property of the family, and while he lived, his adult sons would only receive an allowance (*peliculum*) to support their own households. The dowry represented a significant supplement to this income. Aristocratic men who had fallen on hard times might seek wives who came with a substantial sum to her name. "But tell me why is Censennia, on her husband's testimony, the best of wives?" Juvenal snipes, "She brought him a million sesterces."[29]

Marriage was not a binding legal institution, but rather a mutual agreement made privately between a couple and their two families. As a result, terminating the association was a fairly straightforward matter. All that was required was for one or the other spouse to make their intentions known publicly before witnesses. Divorce was particularly common among the rich and powerful, who frequently needed to shift alliances in Rome's changeable political climate. In leaving her husband, however, a woman also left behind any children from that marriage, as they belonged to their father and his family.

While the rules and expectations governing women's lives were restrictive, in actual practice, it became increasingly possible to exercise a degree of autonomy from within the bounds of Roman custom and law. Although a woman was supposed to forever be subordinate to a man, be he father, husband, or guardian, evidence for a number of high-profile and fairly independent women around the end of the Republic suggests an incremental loosening of constraints in the last two centuries B.C. The widowed Cornelia, famed Mother of the Gracchi, was able to refuse a royal suitor, supervise her own estate, and see to the careers of her few remaining children, all seemingly without significant male interference.

At the end of the first century B.C., and in the next two centuries to follow, the restrictions placed on women were further relaxed through legal measures. Until the early imperial period, women were barred from representing themselves in financial or legal affairs. A *paterfamilias*, or other appointed male guardian, was required to transact any business on her behalf. This could prove an awkward arrangement in a society where a relatively low life expectancy left many to cast their net wide for a suitable custodian. Only one in every two Romans who survived childhood managed to reach the age of fifty and fewer still saw sixty. Families consisting of multiple generations were actually more rare than law and tradition would imply. The image of the autocratic *paterfamilias* lording over the lives of his children and grandchildren was a reality for few. A third of all children lost their fathers by puberty and this many again were fatherless by their mid-twenties. Families were often fragmented and reconstituted from distant kin and relations through marriage.

A woman who survived the perils of childbearing might find she had outlived both father and first husband. Under these circumstances, she could be left in possession of inherited wealth and property but without the means to manage it directly. During the reign of the emperor Augustus, a series of laws were enacted that rewarded women with some autonomy in their later years, provided they had fulfilled their prescribed duties as wife and mother.

Passed by the Senate in 18 B.C., the *lex Julia de maritandis ordinibus* (the Julian Law on the Marriage of the Orders) was intended to encourage marriage and the growth of families, while preserving the class structure. Although it allowed marriage between upper-class men and freedwomen, it specifically forbade senators and their descendants from marrying so far beneath their station. The freeborn were barred from marrying the *infamis*, those of "infamous" repute, such as actors, criminals, and prostitutes.[30] Fathers were required to arrange unions for their daughters and provide dowries. Women still single between the ages of twenty to fifty were financially penalized, as were bachelors between the ages of twenty-five to sixty. A grace period was specified during which a woman was allowed to remain unmarried following the death of her husband (one year) or divorce (six months).[31] The law could be restrictive. Men were overlooked for certain high offices if they failed to wed and kept from receiving their inheritances. It proved a great gain for women, however, as it released them from the requirement for male guardianship if they had already borne three legitimate children who survived beyond infancy.[32] Once achieved, they became *sui iuris*, independent, a status they retained for the rest of their lives that enabled them to conduct business in their own name.

The *lex Julia de adulteriis coercendis* (the Julian Law for the Restraint of Adultery) was passed at the same time as the marital law. What had previously been a personal matter between spouses and families became a criminal offense, punishable by law. It was a very one-sided definition of infidelity, referring only to relations between a married woman and any other man not her husband. Husbands were required to repudiate and bring suit against unfaithful wives within a certain period of time or risk public prosecution themselves as accessories. If caught in the act, the law gave a father the right to kill both his daughter and her lover, and a husband the right to kill the lover, if a slave or *infamis*. A woman convicted of adultery was exiled to an island, forfeited a portion of her dowry and property, and was herself classed among the *infamis*.

It was a common theme in Roman literature to decry the degradation of traditional mores and wax nostalgic about the Good Old Days. On the surface, it would appear that Augustus *'leges Juliae* was the emperor's own attempt at legislating "family values," but Augustus was perhaps less concerned that the general citizenry reproduced themselves legitimately and in adequate numbers than he was that the elite members of society dissipated their wealth between multiple heirs, rather than consolidating it among a powerful few who might pose a threat to his regime.

Women with their own resources who had already gained the respect and independence that came from producing their contribution to the next generation tended to have more of a say in their next marriage or could choose not to remarry at all. Studies have shown that it was uncommon for a Roman woman to remarry after the age of thirty-five.[33] To be a *univira*, a woman who had married (and presumably slept with) only one man in her lifetime, brought with it great respect and was worthy of mention in eulogies and epitaphs, but for those without particularly long-lived husbands, only a few could afford the luxury of an honorable widowhood and opt not remarry.

Women of prominent and affluent families were, of course, better able to exploit the opportunities available than were women of more meager means. History attests to numerous aristocratic women who deftly negotiated the constraints placed on their gender to wield considerable influence. Through their own marriages and those of their children, they parlayed wealth and position to forge political alliances that allowed them access to the corridors of power otherwise denied.

History, however, chronicles only those events and personages historians consider to be of consequence: He who holds the stylus decides. Roman literature was written largely by the male intelligentsia and intended for an audience of their peers. The body of work that has survived the vagaries of time and the biases of subsequent scholarly preservation can hardly be considered to represent the full spectrum of Roman society.

In recent decades, efforts have been made to address these imbalances in the historical record. Archaeology, as well as the study of inscriptions and more ephemeral documents, such as personal letters and contracts, have all been instrumental in shedding light on the underrepresented in ancient literature: the working classes, slaves, children, and particularly, women.

Nowhere is the wide range of roles women played better illustrated than in the doomed town of Pompeii. Nestled in the curve of the Bay of Naples in the Campanian region south of Rome, the area had been a fashionable getaway for society's elite, an escape from the heat and noise and stench of the city. Lavish estates dotted the landscape, while in town could be found all the comforts of Rome, including theaters, temples, baths, and brothels.

Pompeii was literally wiped off the map by the sudden eruption of nearby Mount Vesuvius one late summer's day in A.D. 79. It was a disaster of horrific proportion, carving a path of destruction some seventeen kilometers wide through the heart of the thriving coastal community and ending the lives and livelihoods of thousands who dwelled in the shadow of the sleeping volcano.

Yet, the same cataclysmic forces that devastated a countryside have provided archaeologists with an unparalleled vision of everyday life almost two thousand years ago. Entombed under layer upon layer of volcanic ash and stone, Pompeii was preserved in exceptional condition. Along its ruined streets once walked women of every station and stripe: empress and entrepreneur, priestess and prostitute. In this place, women speak with their own voices and by their own deeds.

One of the area's most famous inhabitants was Poppaea Sabina, second wife of the emperor Nero. The historian Tacitus documents their sordid and indiscreet affair in his *Annals*. Poppaea's father, Titus Ollius, politically disgraced himself when she was not yet a toddler, leading her to be named after her mother's line, the Poppaei, a distinguished Pompeian family. Poppaea was reported to have first caught Nero's eye with her beauty and wiles in A.D. 58. The only complication: They were both married, she to her second husband M. Salvius Otho, a senator and close companion of Nero's, and he to Octavia, daughter of his predecessor, the emperor Claudius. Otho was quickly dispatched to govern the distant province of Lusitania (Portugal) but Nero's union with Octavia was politically important and could not be so easily dismissed. It was not until A.D. 62 that Nero got up the nerve to clear the way to wed his mistress, and by then Poppaea was already pregnant with their first child. He officially divorced Octavia on the grounds of barrenness, but Poppaea still perceived the popular and influential Octavia as a threat. She is said to have goaded Nero into bringing false charges of adultery against his first wife, having her banished and, ultimately, murdered, her head brought back to Rome to reassure Poppaea Octavia was a rival no longer.

Poppaea's own reign as empress was brief. One night in A.D. 65, pregnant with their second child, she made the mistake of chiding her husband for returning home late from the races. In a fit of rage, Nero kicked her, causing her death. Tacitus discounts rumors she was actually poisoned by the emperor, noting Nero's love for Poppaea and his great desire for children. Just two years earlier, Nero had been so elated when she bore him a daughter that he bestowed high honors on both mother and child, held public games in celebration, and decreed the construction of a temple to Fertility. His joy turned to sorrow when the baby died only a few months later.

Flouting convention, he even went so far as to have the infant deified. "The emperor's delight had been immoderate; so was his
mourning," criticized Tacitus.[34]

During her short time in power, Poppaea did not forget her
roots. She is believed to have personally owned and embellished the
sprawling seaside villa in the Pompeii suburb of Oplontis, a property
that had been in her family for more than a century. Like so many of
the magnificent country estates in this part of the Bay of Naples, it
also fell prey to Vesuvius' wrath and lay buried for centuries. Sys-
tematic excavations begun in the 1960s have revealed dozens of
rooms, many adorned with masterful trompe l'oeil frescoes, as well
as formal gardens and a huge swimming pool, some sixty-five meters
in length. Poppaea and members of her family are also associated
with several important properties in Pompeii proper, including the
House of the Menander, a grand town house so named for the painting of the Greek poet found on the wall of the decorated niche at the
back of its peristyle garden. Both of these sumptuously appointed
homes were undergoing extensive renovations at the time of the
eruption, suggesting the family's fortunes survived Poppaea's tragic
demise. In fact, the wealth of the House of the Menander must have
been so well known that an attempt was made, most likely by thieves,
to reach the buried structure in the years following A.D. 79, but the
tunnel collapsed on the unlucky treasure hunters, leaving their bodies to be discovered by archaeologists in the 1930s (along with chests
containing jewelry and 118 pieces of silver plate found in the house's
basement vault.)[35]

Poppaea herself may have been most fondly remembered by the
residents of Pompeii for interceding with the emperor on their
behalf. In A.D. 59, a riot broke out in the stands of Pompeii's

amphitheater between local rowdies and visiting rivals from the neighboring town of Nuceria.[36] Upon hearing of the bloodshed that ensued, Nero, who had only recently become the patron of Nuceria, had Pompeii's beloved stadium closed for gladiatorial contests for a period of ten years. With a Pompeian in the palace, however, some suspect the interdiction did not last the full term.[37] After receiving damage in a major earthquake in A.D. 62, the amphitheater was quickly restored through funds from private donors and, sometime later, a barracks for professional gladiators was established elsewhere in the city. It certainly does not seem the amphitheater remained shuttered and dark for long. Graffiti found on walls around the town are thought to allude to the one responsible for lifting the ban. They hail the decisions of the emperor and empress and wish health and long life to Poppaea, the hometown girl who made good.

While no other woman from Pompeii may have risen to quite the same heights as Poppaea Sabina, others proved equally influential in local affairs. Evidence from excavation and inscriptions reveal women involved in trade and industry, real estate and urban renewal, religion and politics.

Although not a member of the Roman aristocracy like Poppaea, Eumachia also belonged to a well-established Pompeian family from which she inherited considerable wealth and property. Her merchant father, Lucius Eumachius, operated a large brick and pottery works in town. He did a brisk business exporting Pompeian vintages widely throughout the empire. Wine amphora bearing his seal have been found as far as Spain, France, Carthage, and Athens.[38] Upon her father's death, Eumachia may well have taken over the family businesses, managing them with the help of her husband, a prominent local landowner and magistrate. Eumachia's real claim to fame was not in wine and bricks, however, but in how she applied her wealth and position to the benefit of herself, her family, and her community.

Sometime during the early decades of the first century A.D., Eumachia commissioned the construction of an imposing edifice in Pompeii's forum, the town's commercial, religious, and political center. Spanning an entire city block, it stood alongside the most important municipal buildings, including the law courts, halls of government, markets, and temples of Rome's patron deities. Its monumental colonnaded entrance was decorated with intricate marble carvings of the highest quality, and the large interior court-yard was lined with honorary statues. Presiding over all, in a central apse off the colonnaded porch stood the goddess Concord (a divine personification of harmony). This statue may have also been a por-trait of Livia, wife of the first emperor, Augustus, and mother of the second, Tiberius, who was often depicted as the embodiment of Imperial Concord and Piety.[39] The intended purpose of this unusual structure is not clear, but the dedications set above each of its two entrances leave little doubt who was responsible for it. They proclaim that:

Eumachia, the public priestess, daughter of Lucius, had the vestibule, the covered gallery, and the porticoes made with her own money and dedicated in her own name and in the name of her son, Marcus Numistrius Fronto, in honor of the goddesses Concord and Augustan Piety.[40]

It was common practice among the upper echelons of Roman society to compete for public favor through the funding of large-scale civic works. Contributing to the construction or renovation of theaters, baths, and temples enhanced an individual's prestige and brought the kind of recognition needed to make a successful run for political office. With its invocation of an empress and other allusions to the glory and grandeur of Rome, this building attempted to associate its donors with the imperial family in the minds of Pompeii's citizenry. As a woman, Eumachia could not have hoped to reap the benefits of such lofty aspirations herself, but the building's founding does seem to coincide with a bid in local elections by her son, who is also prominently featured in the dedicatory inscriptions.

For this and perhaps other unrecorded accomplishments, a statue was erected in Eumachia's honor by the *fullones*, craftsmen who manufactured and laundered woolen cloth. Now in the National Archaeological Museum of Naples, this slightly larger than life likeness was originally set in a small gallery at the far end of the Eumachia building and depicts the benefactress with the serene countenance, veiled head, and heavy draperies of a pious and modest Roman matron. The inscription on the pedestal reads, "To Eumachia, the daughter of Lucius, the public priestess, from the fullers."[41] The discovery of several *fullonicae*, or laundries, at Pompeii, suggests that the wool trade was an important industry in the town. Eumachia's building has been variously interpreted as a wool market, guildhall, or businessmen's forum, but whatever its intent, at least one influential commercial guild was particularly appreciative of her munificence.

Eumachia herself seems to have risen to as high an office as her birth and gender might allow. Her role as public priestess—possibly in the service of the goddess Venus, divine patroness of Pompeii—must have been a position of great esteem, as the title is frequently mentioned in the epitaphs of other eminent women whose tombs line the roads leading to the town. Not to be forgotten in death as in life, Eumachia also built an impressive funerary monument for herself and her household outside the city walls near the Nucerian Gate.

Eumachia was not the only woman in Pompeii to be recognized for her contributions to the community. Mamia, a contemporary of Eumachia's who was also a *sacerdos publica*, or public priestess, was granted a burial plot in an exclusive location just beyond the Herculaneum Gate by the decurions, the local senate. To what she owed this special honor is not explicitly stated, but an inscription found elsewhere at the site identifies her as the dedicator of a temple to the guardian spirit (*genius*) of the emperor Augustus, which she built "on her own land and with her own money."[42] Mamia's temple is identified as the structure on the east side of the forum next door to the Eumachia building. It was later converted into a shrine to the emperor Vespasian.

While Poppaea, Eumachia, and Mamia made their mark in the political and civic spheres, the extent of a woman's command in the business realm is attested by the house of Julia Felix. Spanning two whole city blocks, this was one of the largest urban villas found in Pompeii. Originally conceived as a single private dwelling, some later reversal of fortune may have forced its owner to open portions of her beautiful home to the public. Converted into a multipurpose establishment, it incorporated several separate living quarters, an orchard and cultivated gardens, a bath suite and shops, many of which were available for lease. A notice posted near an entrance along the Via dell'Abbondanza, one of the town's main thoroughfares, advertises:

For Rent
From August 13, with a 5-year lease
On the property of Julia Felix, daughter of Spurius:
The elegant Venus Baths,
Streetfront shops and booths,
And second-story apartments.[43]

A painted frieze from an entry room off the same street depicts a bustling market day in the Forum. Vendors hawk all manner of wares, from woolen cloth to bronze pots and pans; men and women mingle freely on the street and haggle over the price of goods; two women sit at a sandal-maker's stall trying on shoes, while another pauses to give alms to a beggar. These lively, crowded scenes capture the busy commercial life of the town, in which both men and women actively participated.[44] By comparison, the long portico and formal garden that lay at the heart of Julia Felix's complex, with their water features, shaded pergola, and marble-pillared porch, must have seemed a cool and quiet oasis for a woman whose home was her business.

Letting out property for commercial use may have been considered a socially acceptable source of income for society's elite, but small family-run enterprises often required the direct involvement of all members of a household, male and female, young and old, free and enslaved. At Pompeii, the division between the domestic and production spheres can be blurred. Evidence for cottage industries may be found in structures that seem to have been originally conceived as private dwellings, from the large-scale fulling works that completely overtook one residence[45] to much more modest endeavors, such as spinning and weaving, which were sometimes done by the women and male slaves of the house as piecework. While some homes were converted to serve as workshops, some shops also incorporated living quarters, single rooms, or small apartments above, behind, or beside a storefront.

It may have been a hallmark of wealth and status to be a lady of leisure, but not all merchants' wives were able to afford the luxury of idleness. In addition to overseeing the daily concerns of the household, they worked alongside their husbands in retail shops, potteries, and bakeries, and some continued to manage the family business on their own in their widowhood. A relief from Ostia portrays a proprietress serving customers from behind the counter of a produce shop. Another carving, now in the Dresden Museum, shows a butcher's wife seated in a high-backed chair keeping the accounts while her husband cuts meat nearby. In Pompeii, a wall painting found outside the shop of the cloth merchant Vecilius Verecundus depicts various aspects of a busy dyeing operation, but it is a woman who sits at the front desk, attending to a female client.

In a portrait from the House of Terentius Neo, an ambitious, upwardly mobile bourgeois couple is pictured in their very best attire. He wears a toga, a symbol of rank and privilege, and she is swathed in a richly dyed mantle. The house is adjacent to a bakery and it is surmised that the two in the painting are the baker and his wife. If so, there is no indication of their occupation in the portrait. The man grasps a rolled scroll and the woman holds a folded writing tablet in one hand and raises the tip of a stylus to her mouth with the other, attributes meant to allude to the erudition and refinement of this aspiring pair. The woman's writing implements, like those used by the butcher's wife in the Dresden relief, may also indicate she is a competent tradeswoman, adept at balancing the books for both household and business.

Businesswomen involved in much less respectable ventures are also represented at Pompeii. Graffiti found in some of the town's over one hundred hotels, inns, and bars indicate women served as waitresses and managers in these (often rather disreputable) establishments. Scrawled on the walls in the hands of both the female staff and the male patrons, the language of their messages is spirited and bawdy, reflecting the tone of these neighborhood watering holes. A series of small vignettes painted on the walls of one such inn reads like a typical night on the town: Two men are served wine by a waitress, then engage in a game of dice, but quarrel over the results of a roll until, finally, they are turned out on their ear by the innkeeper.

One of the best-preserved examples of a Pompeian tavern was possibly owned or operated by a woman. From the open frontage, warmed wine and food could be ladled out to customers from large ceramic jars embedded in the broken marble countertop. Behind the counter, the shop's till was found, still containing the day's proceeds, as were wine amphorae filled with domestic and imported vintages stacked against the wall two and three deep, waiting to be decanted. The name Asellina appears repeatedly in the graffiti on the walls, along with those of many of her wait staff. Although possibly slaves and, as women, unable to vote even if free, they must have believed their opinions carried some weight: Campaign messages painted outside the eatery by barmaids Aegle and Zmyrina urge passersby to support the candidates they favor in local elections.[46]

Amidst the price lists and patrons' tabs recorded on the tavern walls one can find the accounts of small-time pawnbroker Faustilla[47] and boasts of amorous exploits by both women and men. Venues for drinking and gambling, these street-side dives would not normally have been frequented by "decent" folk, and there is some suggestion that the women who did work in these places offered more for sale than just a cup of wine and a hot meal.

There is no question what was for sale in a small two-story building just a short walk from the forum. Located in a seamy part of town behind one of the major public bathhouses, Pompeii's notorious *lupanar*, or brothel, sits at the narrow intersection of two winding streets. Taken from the Latin for she-wolf (*lupa*), the Romans are said to have had more euphemisms for sellers of sexual favors than almost any other profession. Although at one time there was thought to be several dozen such houses of ill repute located all over town, this is the most complete and incontestable.[48] Graffiti by both patron and prostitute practically cover its whitewashed walls, most as graphic and crude as the place itself.

Here was the sex trade at its most unglamorous and squalid. The ground floor consisted of five dark and airless cubicles, each barely large enough to accommodate a purpose-built stone bed. In a frieze running around the central hall, young and healthy couples enthusiastically engage in intercourse on clean linens and mattresses—romanticized images unlikely to be found on the other side of these thresholds. The girls who worked for Africanus and Victor (the brothel's last owners before Vesuvius closed it down for good) were likely slaves. Although men of the upper classes were known to frequent such establishments, their clientele probably consisted mainly of those on the lowest rungs of the social ladder, other slaves and freedmen who spent what little they earned to buy into the painted fictions above the doors.[49]

At Pompeii, the names and achievements of a handful of women of wealth and privilege were commemorated for all to see on inscribed marble sepulchers in the crowded *necropoli* outside the city gates. At the opposite end of the social spectrum, graffiti scratched into plaster walls affords a fleeting glimpse into the lives of some whose names were immortalized by a chance combination of vandalism and cataclysm. Yet, comparatively few women received such real or dubious honors.

Unrecorded are the names of the thousands of others who lived, labored, and loved in this ancient town, women who worked in the home and in Pompeii's multitude of workshops, who shopped along the Via dell'Abbondanza, luxuriated in the public baths, attended games at the amphitheater, and brought offerings to the temple of Venus. Here, archaeology takes up the stories of this anonymous majority, constructing a picture of women's daily lives through the items they left behind: cook pots and table wares, spindle whorls and loom weights, jewelry, hand mirrors, perfume bottles, cosmetic kits, and writing cases. Together with the insights provided by inscriptions, art, and architecture, these artifacts attest to the varied nature of women's experience.

Whether highborn or low, rich, poor, free, or enslaved, the tragedy of A.D. 79 did not discriminate. Poppaea, Eumachia, and Mamia did not live to see the demise of their cherished town, but the fates of Julia Felix, Asellina and her politically minded barmaids, and Africanus and Victor's girls are unknown. They may have been witnesses to the catastrophe or even its victims.

It is estimated that some two thousand people perished at Pompeii, many more in addition in outlying villas and neighboring towns. The region around Mount Vesuvius was long known to be seismically active. In his *Naturales Quaestiones*, the philosopher Seneca even remarked on the frequency of tremors in Campania in his discussion of the highly destructive earthquake of A.D. 62 that damaged and destroyed buildings down the length of the Bay of Naples. Vesuvius itself had lain dormant for a millennium and local inhabitants probably felt they had little to fear from this mountain on whose fertile slopes they tended their vineyards.

All this was to change on the morning of August 24, A.D. 79. Sometime before noon, residents of Pompeii were rocked by a violent explosion. The area had experienced a number of small quakes in recent days, but this was altogether different. Looking to the mountain peak that had always loomed above their town, they watched in horror as it erupted into a dark and ominous column shooting tens of kilometers into the air. From his relatively safe vantage in Misenum at the northernmost tip of the bay, Pliny the Younger watched this terrible event unfold and lived to write about it in two letters to Tacitus.[50] He describes a rising cloud in the shape of an umbrella pine, with a long narrow trunk and broad, mushrooming canopy.[51]

Pliny's uncle, Pliny the Elder, noted natural scientist and admiral of the fleet, set sail from Misenum to observe the phenomenon firsthand and render assistance to those along the coast. A Roman lady had just sent word she was trapped in her villa at the base of the volcano and doubtless many others were now looking desperately to the water as their only means of escape. By this time, the white-hot pumice and ash Vesuvius had spewed into the sky were falling to earth. The elder Pliny found he could not land anywhere along the shores closest to the volcano and was forced to steer a course many kilometers to the south. Even after arriving at a friend's seaside villa near Stabiae, he was not out of danger.

Prevailing winds drove the majority of the material ejected from the volcano south and west, blanketing a large area that included both Pompeii and Stabiae. Showers of small volcanic stones, or *lapilli*, rained down on the panicked populace. The air was thick with choking dust and ash, blotting out the sun, turning day to night. The younger Pliny reports that some resorted to tying pillows to their heads to protect against the unrelenting hail of stones.

In Pompeii, accumulating ash and *lapilli* collapsed roofs on those who sought shelter. Fires broke out. The town was buried in meters of volcanic debris and, still, it continued to fall throughout the night. Those who would not or could not escape already were in danger of becoming trapped in their own homes and tried to weather the storm by climbing above the rising levels. Their attitude may have been similar to that of Pliny the Elder who, although the sea surged and roiled and fire and lightning could now be seen emanating from the truncated cone of the volcano, opted to have a bath, a meal, and set off for bed—for, surely, the situation could not get any worse.

In the early morning hours of August 25, the worst happened. In a series of pyroclastic explosions, Vesuvius leveled the surrounding landscape. The violent discharges sent high-velocity waves of superheated gases, dust, and stone roaring down the slopes and through Pompeii, shearing off the upper stories of buildings and suffocating and burning all living things that remained. Even as far north as Misenum, the shocks were felt and ash fell like a thick blanket of snow, causing the younger Pliny and his mother to flee to open country. There they survived unharmed, but Pliny the Elder was not so lucky. The edge of the final pyroclastic flow seems to have extended as far south as Stabiae. The older man was overcome by the noxious fumes and collapsed on the beach outside his friend's villa.

Pliny's account of the recovery of his uncle's body describes him as seeming as a man asleep, but the hundreds of bodies recovered from Pompeii suggest the last moments of most victims were hardly peaceful. Huddled against walls and in cellars, some were found alone, others in groups, among them slaves in chains, women in their finery, and babes in arms. Some appear to be families, others the servants and staff of a household, and some just desperate folk thrown together by circumstance. Their torment is made disturbingly real as a result of a casting technique developed by nineteenth-century archaeologists that has captured many of these wretched souls in their final repose.

Pompeii's dead were encased in ash where they fell, leaving behind faithful impressions in the material as it hardened around them. Preserved are such minute details as the folds in their clothes, the straps of their sandals, hairstyles, even the agonized expressions on their faces. A watchdog left forgotten and tethered by its owners is forever frozen in a horrifically contorted position after it reached the length of its chain and was no longer able to stay above the mounting ash. Elsewhere, a young woman was found lying facedown, her tunic drawn to her mouth in an effort to not breathe in the choking air.

It is the same tragic story throughout. A woman and her young daughter attempt to flee out a cellar skylight, but get no farther than their own garden before succumbing. A group of eighteen women and children perish where they took cover in the Villa of Diomedes just outside the city walls. A master (*dominus*) tries to get away to safety with his adored slave girl (*ancilla*), upon whom he lavished expensive gifts, only for them to be struck down together.[52] Outside the House of Sallust, a well-dressed woman falls with her three female attendants, spilling her hurriedly collected valuables out onto the street.

In the Gladiators' Barracks, where over sixty died, the skeleton of a woman was said to have been found, bedecked in jewels, lying in a small cell beside the remains of a man. Who was this mystery women? Was she simply seeking a convenient refuge in her final hours or did she have reason for being in the barracks? One theory is that she could have been high-priced concubine on contract from one of Pompeii's more upscale establishments, or a would-be Eppia, only too late abandoning her life of privilege for the arms of her warrior lover. How many others among the fallen here may have been women? Could there have been a gladiatrix in their midst?

Unfortunately, when the barracks were unearthed in the eighteenth century, excavators could scarcely anticipate the wealth of information archaeologists can now glean from bare bones. In addition to past injuries, age, gender, nutrition, and health all leave their mark on the skeleton. The bodies recovered from the gladiator's quarters would have had much to tell about the lifestyles of the professional fighters found there, but their bones have long since been lost among the scores of Vesuvius' other victims that lie in jumbled heaps in Pompeii's storerooms. We will have to look elsewhere to learn about the lives of gladiators.

Why doesn't he do something? Camilla's father stood frozen, staring, like a cornered animal. He seemed deaf to the din all around him. The waiting was unbearable, but before she let out a scream of her own, someone in his entourage—a pinched and graying dignitary, no doubt an honored guest—leaned over and gave the dazed man a nudge. His reverie broken, he cast about for a verdict.

As sponsor of the games, Camilla and Myrine's fates were in his hands, but her father was never one to go against the crowd, that much had not changed. The audience's approval was audible as he signaled for their lives to be spared—much to the disappointment of the referees, who had been standing behind the two women, ready to make them continue the fight to the death.

Attention quickly drifted to those locked in combat elsewhere in the ring. As Camilla turned toward the exit, she could see Rufus's face in the shadows just inside the tunnel. He was not happy.

Nor did he hide his displeasure. Even though the rest of his "girls" were still performing, the troupe's owner dragged Camilla around backstage, intent on selling her to the first animal handler who would have her. But the day's festivities had woefully depleted their stocks, and when he found the best he could hope for was to have her pecked to death by an ill-tempered ostrich, Rufus decided the willful little gladiatrix was probably worth more to him alive.

They returned to the local gladiator school that had agreed to house Rufus's small company. Because of the gender of his fighters, they had been relegated to a stable behind the main building. Heraklia was already there, having her wounds tended to by one of the house physicians. Rufus was always too cheap to travel with one of his own.

"Here," she said, angrily throwing her palm frond prize in Camilla's face. "This belongs to you! Of all the stupid . . ."

"It worked, didn't it?"

"But you didn't expect it to. Not for you, anyway."

She wanted an explanation, demanded one, deserved one. And, at that moment, Camilla wanted nothing more than to break down and tell her everything, but just then, a flushed and flustered Rufus burst into the room.

"You," he said, pointing a stubby finger at Camilla, "have been requested."

Behind him in the doorway, they could see the silhouette of a gentleman in a toga. Camilla knew who it must be. Heraklia, however, jumped to a very different conclusion and was on her feet.

"No, Rufus, not like this—you swore you'd never do this!"

Camilla put a hand on her shoulder. "It's all right," she said, and whispered the truth in Heraklia's ear.

Looking back, Camilla could see the mixture of surprise and concern on her friend's face as the door closed between them.

❈ 4 ❈

THE LIFE OF A GLADIATOR

Gladiators were the superstars of their day. Rome had its share of famous actors and athletes, politicians and poets, but none captured the hearts and minds of the people like those who fought bravely and died well. These celebrated warriors, instantly recognizable in their trademark arms and armor, were immortalized in painting, mosaic, and sculpture. They were an equally familiar sight of everyday life, a popular decorative motif on common household items such as lamps, bowls, jugs, and knife handles. A real fan might even bring home a souvenir of a day well spent at the games: a small mold-blown glass cup, emblazoned with the names and tiny images of famous fighters of the age.

Gladiators were also a favorite subject of graffiti. More than a few scenes of combat adorn the walls of both public and private buildings at Pompeii. Although only crudely scratched into the plaster, these rough drawings manage to convey all the action and drama of the arena. Pairs of fighters lunge at each other, knees bent, shields up, weapons poised. They are shown in the heat of battle, at the moment of defeat, and celebrating their victory. In one graffito, a gladiator proudly brandishes a palm frond, the champion's reward. In another scene from a house, two unarmed fighters, their shields lying abandoned on the ground, reach out to one another after a battle. One has already been declared the winner and wears upon his head the *corona*, a wreath of laurel leaves, the most coveted of accolades.[1]

From the detail in which these scenes were rendered, it is clear their unknown scrawlers took pains to distinguish between the different categories of gladiator and their equipment. Some images appear to commemorate actual events, identifying both contestants by name and listing their vital statistics—the number of bouts fought and won—beside each figure. The result of the pairing depicted is also noted with a "V" for the victor and an "M" for *missio*, if the loser's life was spared. In this way, a wall at Pompeii records the impressive debut of one Marcus Attilius, a *tiro*, trained but untried, who bested two seasoned gladiators in rapid succession. His very first opponent was Hilarus, who had lost only one of fourteen prior fights. The two are shown charging toward each other, swords drawn, but the notation by Attilius' name declares him the winner. In a second sketch, close by the first, the story continues: No longer considered a *tiro* in his second appearance in the arena, Attilius was pitted against another experienced fighter, Lucius Raecius Felix, unbeaten in twelve contests, but again Attilius prevailed. The graffito depicts the moment when Raecius Felix admitted defeat, throwing down his helmet and bending on one knee before the victorious challenger. Although neither of Attilius' initial forays ended in death (both his opponents were granted *missio*) other images leave little doubt as to the seriousness of the stakes.

In a graphic fourth century A.D. mosaic now in the Galleria Borghese in Rome, the bodies of the dead and dying litter the ground. Shields and weapons tumble from gladiators' lifeless hands as their adversaries stand over them, poised to deliver the final blow or already exulting in their triumph. Beside the heads of most of the fallen is the Greek letter *theta*, short for *thanatos*, the word for death. To modern sensibilities, so many lives lost for the mere sake of entertainment seems incomprehensible, but to Romans, such scenes of carnage were a deeply entrenched part of the culture. Few expressed a genuine distaste for the games. Many more flocked to the amphitheater and eagerly followed the exploits of their favorite performers.

Who were these men and women who risked their lives for the amusement of others? The Romans, while not the originators of the gladiatorial contest, wholeheartedly embraced the concept early on in their history, staging fights between foreign captives or slaves as part of the funeral ceremonies for important personages beginning in the mid–third century B.C. In a macabre game of one-upmanship, what began as simple duels between a few pairs quickly escalated into the hundreds as influential families competed with one another to give their members a more lavish and bloody send-off than the last. Gladiator schools were soon established to keep pace with the ever-growing demand for skilled competitors. In this environment of institutionalized butchery, fighting styles became more refined and formalized, requiring combatants of particular quality. Though still mostly drawn from the ranks of prisoners of war and slaves, true gladiators developed into highly trained professionals. Honing their deadly talents between matches, those who survived to fight again became increasingly accomplished and sought after.

Training and maintaining a proper gladiator was a costly endeavor, a risky investment that could disappear at a sword's stroke. Consequently, the majority of the unfortunates who ended up in the amphitheater were deemed expendable: prisoners and criminals condemned to be cut down by half-starved animals (*ad bestias*) or by the sword (*ad gladium*), often wielded by other, equally desperate captives and convicts. These were public executions—base entertainment at best—scheduled at times of the day when the bulk, or at least the more discerning, of spectators might be occupied with other business, such as at midday. These gruesome exhibitions are not to be mistaken for actual gladiatorial combat, which adhered to strict forms, rules, and rituals.

Among the offenses that carried a sentence of death in the arena were arson, murder, treason, and the desecration of temples. Depending upon the severity of the transgression and the status of the individual, however, a person could instead be sentenced to a life (albeit a short one) of forced labor, either toiling in the mines (*ad metallum*) or training at a gladiator school (*ad ludum*). Both were considered virtual death sentences, but conditions in the state-run mines were so abysmal that to be condemned to become a gladiator was in some ways preferable. In the arena, at least, one stood a fighting chance, however slim.

Slaves who could not be controlled were of little use to their owners. Masters who did not care to execute them by their own hand had the right to send their recalcitrant property to their death in the amphitheater. A guest at Trimalchio's banquet in the *Satyricon* gleefully gossips about Glyco who, after discovering his trusted, but enslaved, steward in a compromising position with the lady of the house, was planning to turn the man over to the beasts, even though it meant making the affair public.[2] When a fugitive slave was recaptured, it was up to the owner, as head of household, to decide their punishment, but when owners could not be located, runaways were often sold off cheaply to perform backbreaking labor in trades where the turnover rate was high, such as at the gladiator schools. In his biography of the emperor Vitellius, who reigned very briefly in A.D. 69, Suetonius recounts one point during his tumultuous on-again-off-again relationship with his slave and later freedman, Asiaticus, when Vitellius sold him to an itinerant trainer of gladiators, only to buy him back just before his first match.[3] During his reign in the early second century A.D., the emperor Hadrian made some attempt to curb the whim of abusive masters by requiring them to give good cause before allowing them to sell a slave, male or female, to a brothel keeper or gladiator trainer.[4]

The composition of the gladiator population was a reflection of the times.[5] During the late republic and early imperial period (also known as the Principate) Rome saw great influxes of war captives as a result of successful military campaigns in distant lands. Later, as the rate of expansion slowed, the flow of defeated enemies into the amphitheater was also reduced to a trickle. Criminals and slaves bought at auction or received from disgruntled owners likely made up the shortfall. Whatever the source, all had one thing in common: They were society's dregs, marginalized figures with no rights under Roman law and little say in their own destinies. For them, the arena held the thin hope of freedom at the end of a successful career.

Whether captives, criminals, or slaves, in the eyes of Roman audiences those who appeared in the amphitheater were all deserving of their plight. By resisting Rome's rule, flouting its laws, or disobeying their masters, they had denied the state's rightful preeminence and the fundamental authority of the *paterfamilias*. Public executions symbolically reinforced this worldview and reassured spectators of their own social and political superiority. To allow someone to train and fight as a gladiator was, compared to outright execution, seen to be an act of compassion, providing a person the opportunity to redeem him or herself through mortal combat.

Given these attitudes it seems incredible that anyone would take on this deadly profession by choice, but evidence suggests many did. Several gladiators' epitaphs bear the unmistakable *tria nomina* of Roman citizens. Some were driven by dire circumstance to sign away their lives: destitute freeborn and freed individuals who had run out of options. Others found their skills singly suited to the arena, such as retired gladiators who, even after having won their liberty, often returned to the only occupation they knew. It has also been suggested that daughters of gladiators may have followed in the family business, having received expert instruction from their retiree fathers.[6] Then there were the bored nobles, even the occasional emperor, who took up the sword, much to the horror and derision of their peers. Although their actual numbers must have been comparatively few, these restive and reckless aristocrats garnered a disproportionate amount of attention from the historians and satirists among their fellows.

The degradation of Roman values is the central theme in the works of Juvenal. He repeatedly bemoans the depths to which patricians would sink by appearing on the stage and, worse, in the amphitheater. In addition to the upper-class ladies who liked to play at being gladiators, a performance in the arena by a descendant of a once proud aristocratic line is also met with a sneer:

> *Here, too, public scandal awaits you: a Gracchus fighting,*
> *and not in full armor, either, with target and falchion—*
> *such gear he can't abide (but condemns and detests it:*
> *no visor to cover his face). What he wields is—a trident!*
> *Once he's gathered his net, and thrown it, with a flick of the wrist,*
> *and missed his cast, his face exposed to the spectators,*
> *quite recognizable, he bolts for dear life from the arena.*[7]

By volunteering to serve as gladiators, Roman citizens relinquished that most precious of possessions: their freedom. This was the prize Amazon and Achillia, the two female gladiators of the Halicarnassus relief, fought for and won, but which many others died without ever having attained. Those who committed to this life willingly (*auctorati*) were little better than slaves themselves, joining the *infamis* class of outcasts and surrendering their bodies—indeed, their very lives—to the owner of the troupe for the duration of their contract. For that period of servitude they would swear a solemn oath, in effect agreeing to be "burnt with fire, shackled with chains, whipped with rods, and killed with steel."[8] Yet, in spite of these apparent indignities, so many highborn sons and daughters rushed to disgrace themselves in the amphitheater that emperors felt compelled to enact legislation to stem the tide.

Fame, fortune, and glory: These were the enticements. Like the prizefighters of today, a gladiator at the top of his or her profession might command a substantial sum for their appearance, fighting only a few times a year and winning the adulation of the crowd, not to mention a hefty purse if they came away the winner. Evidence suggests that veteran fighters were repeatedly lured back to the arena with the promise of a substantial bonus upon the completion—that is to say, survival—of their renewed contracts. Although allegedly no great fan of the games and a bit of a cheapskate when it came to public expenditures, the emperor Tiberius was said to have paid ex-gladiators one thousand gold pieces each for a single return performance.[9]

The life of a gladiator may have also offered other, more mundane advantages for individuals who had fallen on hard times. Those with citizen rights but little else to show for it could barter their independence in exchange for structure and discipline, regular meals, and medical treatment.[10] In this way, their daily existence might not have been so different from that of a common foot soldier in the Roman army, with a contractual length of service considerably shorter than the requisite twenty to twenty-five years of the military. At times, the odds of survival in the arena may have seemed better than the infantry. If they performed well, an audience could show a gladiator mercy in defeat. Such clemency was unlikely to be found on the battlefield.

Although express references to the careers of women gladiators are few and far between, what hints and clues have survived suggest their situation may have differed little from their male counterparts. Amazon and Achillia, for example, competed as seasoned professionals, using standard gladiatorial equipment, and proved impressive enough in their accomplishments to be commemorated in stone. How they lived and trained, however, can only be a matter of conjecture, based on what is known about gladiators in general.

Whether sentenced or sold into the life or entering into it voluntarily, new recruits became part of a troupe, known as a *familia gladiatoria*. These companies usually bore the name of the owner—sometimes the emperor himself—whose authority echoed that of a *paterfamilias* over his household slaves. Organizations ranged in size from small traveling bands under private management to the sprawling gladiator mills of Rome where occupants could range into the thousands. Hard and uncompromising, these institutions may have nevertheless provided their members with a sense of belonging and purpose that, as social misfits and pariahs, they might otherwise have been denied. Like soldiers in a barracks, gladiators lived together at a school (*ludus*), ate and trained as a unit, even banded together to cover the funeral expenses of one of their own.[11] But whatever camaraderie might develop was tempered by the knowledge that, for the members of these so-called "families," survival depended upon the death of their fellows, usually by their own hand, as gladiators from the same group were often set to fight against one another.

Most *ludi*, especially the four imperial centers in Rome, were large and complex ventures, requiring a sizable staff to run. It was quite possible, however, for a school's entire population to consist of slaves or freedmen, some still in the service of their former master, the establishment's owner. This included the team physician, smiths, and trainers, as well as the manager of the school himself. Despite their lowly status, a rigid hierarchy was observed within the walls of the *ludus*, even amongst the gladiators.

As most new arrivals came to a school under duress, these raw "recruits" were required to prove their fidelity over time. Novices practiced with wooden or blunted swords against straw effigies or wooden targets and were not trusted with sharpened blades until the moment they entered the arena. Those who resisted the strict routine and strenuous training could expect to be harshly disciplined. In the Gladiator Barracks at Pompeii, some individuals were found in cells shackled in leg irons, unable even to stand fully upright.

Once determined sufficiently schooled to fight publicly, the novice became a *tiro* and quickly advanced to the status of *veteranus* upon survival of his first fight, a not insignificant achievement. In addition to tallying every fight and win, by the end of the first century A.D. gladiators had begun to mark their seniority with the rank of *palus*. The title, taken from the word for the stationary post used in sword practice, consisted of four successive honorifics, the foremost being *primus palus*, or first *palus*. This ranking system echoed that of the Roman military, in which the commanding centurion of the leading unit in a legion was known as the *primus pilus*, or first spearman.

A pair of marble tablets found near the Via Labicana outside Rome illustrates that paramilitary overtones extended beyond the *familia gladiatoria* to include more informal organizations.[12] Dating to A.D. 177, the inscription catalogs the names and fortes of the members of one particular *collegium* of gladiators dedicated to the service of the god Silvanus. Its thirty-two members are divided into *decuriae*, a term used in the Roman cavalry to denote a squad of ten men. As applied to gladiators, these appear to have been units of similarly proficient fighters. A few members of staff—presumably noncombatants—are also mentioned among the names of gladiators, indicating their relative status within the group. While the first set of ten consisted entirely of veteran gladiators, the second was predominantly *tirones*, but was headed by a veteran and included a masseur and a maker of gladiators' arm guards (*manicarius*). The third *decuria* was a mix of *tirones* and men with no listed fighting specialty, presumably novices and perhaps additional staff. The fouth *decuria* was incomplete and may have represented an entry level from which trainees would rise as they gained seniority and positions came available in the higher tiers. One of the two, however, is identified as a *paegniarius*, a comic gladiator, whose job it was to entertain the audience at intervals between bouts, and whose path of advancement in the troupe likely differed from those who fought in earnest.

A school's accommodations may have also reflected the stratified nature of the *familia*. Whereas conditions for the majority were undoubtedly grim, success did have its perks. In the Ludus Magnus (Great School), the largest of the four imperially owned schools at Rome, it is suggested that occupants were divided by rank and housed in different sections, or Halls.[13] Begun at the end of the first century A.D. by the emperor Domitian and completed by his successors, this *ludus* was the companion piece to the Colosseum, just next door. A subterranean passage linked the two vast structures, enabling the performers to come and go out of the sight of the public. The four sides of the school's main building were lined with cells, most cramped and windowless. At its center was a large practice field built to emulate the greater elliptical arena across the street, complete with rows of raked seating sufficient for upward of a few thousand spectators. Outbuildings included a forge and armory for the manufacturing and storage of the huge arsenal of weapons needed to arm the approximately two thousand gladiators in residence.

Although on a much smaller scale than the Ludus Magnus, the Gladiator Barracks at Pompeii is strikingly similar in its basic plan. Located some blocks away from the amphitheater, the building was originally conceived as a *quadriporticus,* a scenic colonnaded ambulatory and open square that served the surrounding Theater District. However, the two-story structure with its rows of small chambers proved ideally suited for conversion into secure lodgings. Similar to many modern prisons, each cell had a single door opening out onto the long walkway that surrounded the central courtyard. Movement around the building could be easily monitored and controlled. Although early excavations did not record whether these cells were differentially appointed, it is known that of the more than sixty individuals who perished here in A.D. 79 some were abandoned to their fate in chains while another entertained a finely dressed lady during his last moments.

Sponsors of games (*editores*) were not required to maintain their own personal stable of performers. These could be hired for the occasion from owners who made a tidy sum leasing out their private stock. In a letter to Atticus, Cicero suggests the fighters his friend purchased could have quickly paid for themselves:

> My word! You have bought a fine troop. I hear your gladiators are fighting splendidly. If you had cared to let them out, you would have cleared your expenses on those two shows.[14]

Profiting from those who put their bodies on display for money was, of course, a most unseemly occupation for a Roman aristocrat. Nevertheless, some very prominent men are known to have possessed large troupes of gladiators, including Julius Caesar and Marc Antony. During the Principate, provincial priests of the Imperial Cult kept gladiators for shows they were expected to mount in honor of the emperor, while the emperor himself became the exclusive proprietor of all four major gladiator schools in Rome. To avoid taint from this sordid business, many private citizens portrayed themselves as mere fanciers of the games, who just happened to collect gladiators as a sideline or hobby. The lives of these men and women were by no means their primary source of income, or so they would have others believe.

Affluent owners left the administration of day-to-day affairs to a hireling, known as a *lanista*, who consequently bore the brunt of the social stigma. They oversaw every aspect of the business from the recruitment and procurement of able bodies to the negotiation of prices for a company's appearance. They managed the *ludus*, saw to the fighters' training regimen, traveled with the troupe on the road, and even handled the promotion for events on occasion. The term for this profession, like the games themselves, is thought by many to have its origins among the Etruscans who inhabited the territory just north of Rome. Its derivation from the Etruscan word *lanius*, or butcher, gives some indication of how these figures were regarded. Roman literature and law are quite explicit on the subject, classing *lanistae* with other traffickers in human flesh. Like pimps and their prostitutes, they shared the status of *infamis* alongside their gladiators. Martial, who is attributed with a collection *On the Spectacles* in which he waxes rhapsodic about the games held in the Colosseum, considered *lanistae* among the worst of humanity. In an epigram insulting a critic and frequent source of ire named Vacerra, the poet calls the man, among others things, an informer, slanderer, swindler, and a *lanista*.[15]

These shady entrepreneurs sometimes worked on behalf of one

or more owners with whose gladiators they had been entrusted, but many owned some or all of their stock outright. Their activities, however, seem to have become increasingly constrained and regulated over time. While the revenues may have been seen to be awash with human blood, the emperors were not above demanding their share of the profits from this extremely lucrative industry. They appointed agents, *procuratores*, to supervise the *lanistae* and ensure all proper taxes were collected on their dealings. Never to be outdone, emperors often needed fighters by the thousands for their grandiose spectacles. They quickly learned to cut out the middleman and became both chief consumer and supplier of gladiators in Rome. The independent *lanistae* were effectively squeezed out of the capital, which had been their largest market, but seem to have made up for the loss in the provinces.

The *Aes Italicense*, a bronze tablet found at the Roman city of Italica in southern Spain, provides scholars with a window through which to view the relationship between *lanistae* and the state. Dating to sometime around A.D. 177, during the reign of Marcus Aurelius, it records efforts to curtail price gouging by this nefarious group, who are portrayed as a necessary evil: despicable profiteers, but indispensable nonetheless. In return for some tax forgiveness, specific upward limits were set on the overall cost of shows and the fees a *lanista* could charge for his gladiators' services. According to the text, these measures were enacted following a desperate entreaty by a delegation from the Gallic provinces who had come to find the skyrocketing costs of games too much to bear. One example is given of a new priest of the Imperial Cult who had all but given up his inheritance for lost when he learned of his appointment, certain that it would all go to meeting the *lanistae*'s flagrantly inflated prices. Amounts were set for gladiators on a sliding scale based on their quality, the size of the event, and the relative rank within the empire of the city in which the games were to be held. The best fighters commanded the most impressive sums, including veteran *auctorati*, whose value was on par with gladiators of the highest grade at the most prestigious of games. At the opposite end of the scale were the *gregarii*, who were not featured competitors but instead fought as a group under a standard, or team insignia, at a fraction of what the headliners cost. Also specified was the portion of the prize money gladiators might expect to claim as their own: A quarter of the purse would go directly to the fighter if a free individual under contract, and a fifth if a slave.

Training was the key to a gladiator's survival and success. To build strength and stamina, gladiators, like soldiers, are thought to have drilled with more heavily weighted equipment than was used in actual performances. To hone their technique, practicing against the *palus* with wicker shield and wooden foil was seen by the writer Vegetius as essential for both soldier and gladiator alike:

> Each recruit would plant a single post in the ground so that it could not move and protruded six feet. Against the post, as if against an adversary, the recruit trained himself using the foil and hurdle like a sword and shield, so that now he aimed at, as it were, the head and face, now threatened the flanks, then tried to cut the hamstrings and legs, backed off, came on, sprang, and aimed at the post with every method of attack and art of combat, as though it were an actual opponent. In this training, care was taken that

the recruit drew himself up to inflict wounds without exposing any part of himself to a blow.[16]

Juvenal mockingly describes very similar maneuvers undertaken by women as part of their exercises.[17]

Those with the luck and skill to survive could look forward to treatment akin to that of thoroughbred racehorses. Great care was paid to the health and nutrition of these performers. Owners engaged physicians of the finest quality to look after their investments. In the second century A.D., Galen of Pergamum—one of the most illustrious figures in the world of ancient medicine after Hippocrates—tended to gladiators early in his career before becoming personal physician to the emperor Marcus Aurelius. Masseurs (*unctores*) were also on hand to keep the fighters in condition, and a legion of staff tended to their equipment and needs. In the Gladiator Barracks at Pompeii, the kitchen, dining, and service rooms alone took up most of one side of the building.

Advanced students received specialist training from professional instructors (*doctores*) who were experts in particular types of combat, many having been gladiators themselves. Owners went to great lengths to obtain the best teachers, hoping to improve the caliber of their fighters and, consequently, their asking price. To ensure he had adept fighters for the games under his sponsorship, Caesar sent gladiators to train in the homes of Roman knights and senators skilled at arms, thinking they would receive more individual attention under the tutelage of such prominent men.[18] According to Kathleen Coleman:

So sophisticated were the methods that the gladiators were trained in, that on their epitaphs they specifically mention if they could fight in more than one style. That was something really exceptional, and if you could fight in as many as three styles, you really were superman.

One such multitalented individual is the subject of effusive praise in a poem by Martial. The gladiator Hermes is said to be "skilled in all weaponry," especially the trident and battling spear. A most formidable opponent, he was the terror of other famed fighters and the "gold mine of seat-mongers."[19]

While the masses may not have appreciated the subtle nuances of well-drilled moves and tactics, they knew a good show when they saw it. A few, however, imagined themselves connoisseurs of the "sport" and had more exacting standards. Gladiators who came to the profession of their own accord were thought to be of an overall better quality than those forced into service. A guest at Trimalchio's banquet in the *Satyricon* gleefully informs another:

> We're going to have a holiday with three days' show that's the best ever—and not just a hack troupe of gladiators but freedmen for the most part.[20]

There is no way to tell with certainty what status Great Dover Street Woman enjoyed in life, only that she was greatly revered in death. No weapons were recovered from her burial and no epitaph survives, if ever one existed. How many bouts she may have fought and won, the style in which she might have done battle, these will never be known, but there is a wealth of information on the types of equipment that would have been available for her to use.

Although their very name comes from the Latin word for sword (*gladius*), gladiators offered the crowd a wide variety of arms and fighting forms. Roman audiences developed a taste for the exotic early in the history of the games, believed to have been fueled by the large numbers of foreign captives that flooded into Rome as it began to extend its control throughout Italy and beyond. Forced to fight as gladiators, these prisoners of war appeared in the arena with their own native weapons, and these novel modes of combat and armament eventually became fossilized into distinct types.

One category of gladiator, thought to be among the oldest, was the Samnite. Dwelling along the Apennine Mountains south of Rome, the Samnite people proved both a powerful ally and enemy of Rome. Although content, for a time, to be appeased by treaties and concessions, the Samnite tribes eventually found they could not ignore the upstart city-state's expansionist tendencies and clashed with Rome three times during the mid-fourth to the early third centuries B.C. According to the historian Livy, following a decisive victory in the Second Samnite War (327–304 B.C.), the Roman military commander led a parade of captured arms and armor so spectacular they were used to decorate the Forum in Rome. In a show of contempt against their common enemy, Rome's coastal allies to the south, the Campanians, were also said to have "equipped the gladiators who provided entertainment at their banquets with similar armour and gave them the name of Samnites."[21]

Roman gladiatorial contests were greatly influenced by Campanian practices, if not in fact derived from them.[22] With their characteristic large oblong shield, called a *scutum*, and brimmed helmet with high crest, Samnites cut the most familiar profile of the heavily armed gladiator. They typically fought using the *gladius*, a short, pointed, double-edged sword best suited for thrusting and hacking, which was also a favorite among the Roman legions. In addition to their ornate plumed helm, their armor included one leather or metal greave protecting the left shin, and a heavily padded sleeve, or *manica*, that ran the length of the sword arm, a standard piece of equipment for most gladiators. Although all the rage early on, the Samnite seems to have fallen out of vogue in later centuries, possibly a victim to Roman "political correctness," as the region became so thoroughly subsumed into the empire that its people could no longer be viewed as the foreign "other." This type, however, may have spawned a number of well-known successors from the Principate, such as the *murmillo* and *secutor*, both of whom were equipped with the *scutum* and *gladius*.[23]

Two other fighting forms also took their inspiration from old enemies of Rome: the Gauls and the Thracians. *Gaul* was the term used to refer to the Celtic-speaking inhabitants of much of western Europe north of the Alps. Although viewed as a single people by the Greeks and Romans, they were composed of numerous smaller sovereign units, or tribes. During the fifth century B.C., northern Italy saw successive waves of Gallic migrations, presumably incited by political turmoil in their own lands. Upon their arrival in Italy, the Gauls seemed to have wasted little time in involving themselves in local affairs. They hired themselves out as mercenaries to the various rival factions competing for control of Italy and worked for many of the peninsula states fighting against Rome's ascendancy. The Gauls made a lasting impression on the Roman psyche when, in 390 B.C., they sacked the city itself. Although the Romans eventually beat the invaders back through northern Italy, the incident was still fresh in people's minds almost three and a half centuries later when Julius Caesar waged war against the tribes on their home turf.

How the Roman concept of the Gaulish menace translated to the arena is difficult to determine. No identifiable representations of this early gladiator type survive. In representations of actual Gallic warriors of the period, most are shown with a double-edged iron sword and a large oval or oblong shield with a distinctive vertical metal rib down its center, but very little else. The image of the fearless Gaul wading naked into battle is one echoed in a fifth-century-B.C. Etruscan funerary stele from Bologna and a fourth-century Italic red figure vase now in Bonn. Their strength and nobility, even in defeat, was immortalized by a statuary group from Pergamum erected in the late third century B.C. to celebrate the route of the Galatians, Gauls whose mercenary and migratory expeditions carried them far to the east. Despite having been called "a scourge for everyone" by the writer Polybius,[24] these evocative bronze sculptures portrayed the beaten and dying Gauls with a heroic dignity that must have appealed to Roman tastes, as several figures from the group were later reproduced in marble back in Rome.

Unlike the Gaul, the Thracian, or *thraex*, enjoyed a much longer-lasting popularity as a gladiatorial type and was frequently depicted in art. Their equipment, originally based on that of native warriors from the Balkan region north of the Aegean Sea, is distinguished from other similarly armed gladiators by a high, crescent-shaped crest on their visored helmet, the use of an oddly bent sword (*sica*), and a square shield considerably smaller than the *scutum*. In response to the lesser coverage afforded by their shields, these gladiators also wore more leg protection than most, with padded wrappings similar to the *manica* covering both legs completely, in addition to a pair of greaves on the lower legs.

It was this alternation between protection and exposure that made gladiatorial combat so varied and exciting for the audience. A fighter's extremities, or at least his head and leading arm and leg, were covered by helmet, greaves, and *manica* to ward off most non-lethal, yet debilitating, blows that would otherwise threaten to end a match prematurely and unsatisfactorily. However, except for a loincloth and a broad belt made of leather and metal, most fighters remained stripped to the waist. Unlike soldiers of the time who wore breastplates or mail shirts, gladiators' bared chests were thought to signify their readiness to die.[25]

As fighting forms grew more standardized over time, specific combinations of gladiators came to be preferred, each with weapons especially suited to exploit the weaknesses of their opponent's defenses and armor to counteract their particular brand of attack. For best results, lightly armed, agile combatants were pitted against more encumbered and less maneuverable adversaries. This strategy is most evident in the pairing of the *retiarius* and *secutor*.

The *retiarius*, or net fighter, represented a significant departure from the image of gladiators as heavily armored, sword-wielding warriors. An invention of the first century A.D. and wildly popular throughout the Principate, this was one of the few forms without military parallel, its inspiration instead coming from a most unlikely source: a fisherman. Although the *retiarius*'s genesis is obscure, there was at least one other marine-themed gladiator, the *murmillo*, which took its name from a Greek word for fish and sported a helmet with a high angled crest, resembling a dorsal fin. However, while such a fish-man might seem the natural enemy of the net fighter, the two do not seem to have ever been paired together.

At first glance, the *retiarii* would have appeared rather vulnerable, entering the ring with minimal protection, save for a high shoulder guard (*galerus*) and the ubiquitous *manica*. Both were worn on the left to allow free range of motion of the right arm for the casting of a weighted net large enough to ensnare an opponent. Their only other weapons were a long-handled trident and a dagger that came into play once an adversary was caught up. If the first throw of the net should miss, there was little opportunity to gather it back up for a second try, placing the fighter at a distinct disadvantage. When the battling Gracchus so lamented by Juvenal found himself with just a trident in hand against a fully armed foe, he turned tail and ran.

In an effort to understand the tactical advantages afforded by such a novel set of equipment, scholars and enthusiasts alike have set about faithfully reproducing the gladiator's arms and armor. Often, these reconstructions are based on known ancient examples, such as the veritable treasure trove of helmets, shields, armor, and weapons left behind by the gladiators of Pompeii. Peter Connolly, an authority on Roman military equipment, considers the techniques on which the *retiarius* would have had to rely in combat:

> The *retiarius* did not have a helmet but wore this extended shoulder guard. [The *galerus*] enabled the person to duck their head behind it if a blow was coming straight at their eyes. Also, notice the curve of it, if the blow is coming high towards the level of the eyes it would slide down and not up, again taking it away from the eyes. The eyes were the most important thing because if you were blinded the fight is over and a very good fighter could actually lose their career, which might have lasted for years.

Bareheaded in battle, the *retiarii* were unique among gladiators. They presented a very different face to the audience: their own.

Most fighters in the arena wore all-encompassing helmets that provided vital protection, but also masked their features, transforming their wearers into anonymous juggernauts. The *retiarii*, by comparison, were instantly recognizable, much to Juvenal's dismay. This humanizing element may have contributed to their appeal, but it also set them apart for other, less welcome, distinctions. The emperor Claudius, who took particular interest in the games, was said to have demanded the death of any gladiator who fell while he was in attendance. He was especially keen if the unlucky performers happened to be *retiarii*, for then he could watch the agony of their final moments played out upon their faces.[26]

The customary opponent of the swift and nimble *retiarius* was the heavyset *secutor*, or "pursuer," who did battle with traditional sword and shield. Their helmets, however, appear to have been specifically designed with their adversaries in mind. Unlike the elaborately embellished and high crested headgear of the *thraex* and others, the *secutor*'s helmet was rounded and smooth, almost egg-shaped, with a low curved crest upon which a cast net could gain no purchase. The solid faceplate, with its close-set spaces for the eyes, is seen by some to be vaguely fishlike, but according to Connolly served a much more practical purpose:

Looking normally, if you just stand looking in front of you and can move your eyes, you can see about one hundred and fifty degrees and you are conscious of things actually happening slightly further round than that. When you've got [the *secutor*'s helmet] on it's limited to about one-third of that, fifty degrees is your limit, but the eyes cannot be attacked. The narrow gap between the two eyeholes probably related very much to the trident, so that the trident could not possibly go through and go into the eyes.

Few gladiators clashed with others in their same category. Most of those who did were of unusual types, such as the *equites*, who are believed to have fought at least part of each match on horseback, and the *andabates*, who were very much a specialty act, grappling in full armor and practically blind, the visors on their helmets intentionally obstructing their vision. Another like pairing was the *provocatores* ("challengers"), the category to which Amazon and Achillia are thought to have belonged.

The identification is not incontrovertible, but the two women bear many of the signs of being *provocatrices*. Identically outfitted in pleated and belted loincloths with leather-bound *manicae* on their right arms, they are depicted lunging forward, both poised to strike with their short swords or daggers from behind the protective curve of their long rectangular shields. Their helmets have been cast aside, revealing hair tightly plaited about their heads. The helms depicted at the bottom of the composition correspond well with those worn by *provocatores*, having a wide flange in back to protect the neck and no crest. However, one telltale feature of the type does appear to be missing: a piece of armor plate that covered the collarbone and upper chest. It is difficult to tell due to the coarseness of the relief and the damage it sustained whether Amazon and Achillia wore this characteristic article or whether it was omitted, in art or actuality, perhaps because it would have obscured their gender. Although general categories of gladiator can be easily recognized, variation in the equipment of a particular type was quite common, especially as these highly structured fighting forms evolved over time.

Each combination of gladiator and gear lent itself to different styles of combat, but with centuries in which to hone technique, there came to be preferred attacks and responses for any given situation. Gladiators drilled rigorously, practicing figures and phrases, move and countermove, over and over again, to the point they were sometimes taken to task for fighting too mechanically, too predictably. With a calendar crammed with festival days, many including lavish gladiator shows, Romans had ample opportunity to critique and draw comparisons, as a character in the *Satyricon* shows in his complaints about the dismal show given by one Norbanus:

> He produced some decayed twopenny-halfpenny gladiators, who would have fallen flat if you breathed on them; I have seen better ruffians turned in to fight the wild beasts. . . . One man, a Thracian, had some stuffing, but he too fought according to the rule of the schools. In short, they were all flogged afterwards. How the great crowd roared at them, "Lay it on!" They were mere runaway [slaves], to be sure. "Still," says Norbanus, "I did give you a show." Yes, and I clap my hands at you. Reckon it up, and I give you more than I got.[27]

Spectators demanded variety and enthusiasm from the performers, but above all else, commended bravery in the face of adversity:

> Look at the gladiators, who are either ruined men or barbarians, what blows they endure! See how men who have been well trained prefer to receive a blow rather than basely avoid it! How frequently it is made evident that there is nothing they put higher than giving satisfaction to their owner or to the people! Even

when weakened with wounds they send word to their owners to ascertain their pleasure: if they have given satisfaction to them they are content to fall. What gladiator of ordinary merit has ever uttered a groan or changed his countenance? Who of them has disgraced himself, I will not say upon his feet, but who has disgraced himself in his fall? Who after falling has drawn in his neck when ordered to suffer the fatal stroke? Such is the force of training, practice, and habit.[28]

As Juvenal's tale of the senator's wife attests, these brawny and charismatic men were also much adored by the ladies. They were the "bad boys" of antiquity, broad shouldered embodiments of the danger and excitement of the amphitheater. That Eppia's chosen paramour was a rather poor specimen, with a runny eye and bad arm, did not seem to deter her. She would follow him to the ends of the earth and risk a dangerous sea voyage just to be with him. It did not matter that he was all but washed up; he was a gladiator all the same.[29]

Graffiti from a private house in Pompeii suggest that a gladiator's physical prowess was appreciated off the field as well as on:

Crescens the netter (*retiarius*) of young women by night.[30]
Celadus the Thracian, thrice victor in three fights, makes the girls sigh.[31]

Found among the many other messages scratched into the plaster of the house's walls and columns, Crescens and Celadus also seem to have acquired the titles "masters of the lasses"[32] and "sweethearts' glory"[33] for their exploits. Whether these two were really the heartthrobs so boasted can only be a matter of conjecture, but the fact that they were able to mingle with the ladies at all suggests they enjoyed considerable freedom outside the *ludus*.

Those who met with success (not just in the bedroom but in the arena as well) had the potential to become local celebrities. A select few even went on to become household names the empire-wide. Martial proclaims the versatile Hermes the "favorite fighter of the age,"[34] while an advertisement for a show in Pompeii's amphitheater describes a featured performer as "desired by all the world."[35] Top-quality fighters who survived to have long and illustrious careers could retire wealthy with the knowledge that they had secured a place of respect for themselves and their descendants in a society that had once rejected them.

The aura that surrounded these performers seems to have had a supernatural quality as well, perhaps hearkening back to their early role as the symbolic couriers of souls through the underworld. The blood of a freshly killed gladiator was believed a cure for epilepsy, while dreaming of being a gladiator was thought to have prophetic significance. According to professional dream interpreters of the time, envisioning oneself fighting a Thracian meant the dreamer would marry a "rich, crafty, egotistical woman."[36] The strength and courage of these fighters, their *virtus*, was even seen to extend to the tools of their trade. Weapons were imbued with a kind of magic by association, becoming potent symbols in and of themselves. While a spear that had taken the life of a gladiator was preferred in the ritual parting of the bride's hair, on one of the rare occasions in which two fighters managed to kill each other simultaneously, the emperor Claudius was said to have ordered knives made from their swords for his personal use.[37]

Death was these warriors' constant companion. They spent their days in training to ward it off while learning to deal it to others. Gladiators were the personification of Roman strength and virtue, achieving nobility through action and facing death, when it did come, with honor. The rites of the arena dominated their daily lives, their performances, their very existence. Although gladiatorial contests appear to have lost their original funereal associations over the centuries, these displays continued to hold great importance and meaning for the Roman people. As the times had changed, so had the gladiator's world. What had begun with a handful of slaves fighting at graveside exploded into an entire industry of heavily ritualized spectacle, combining art, theater, and lethal sport.

Heraklia was in the yard with the rest of the troupe, dividing up Agave's meager belongings.

"Not much to show for a long career," said Myrine, poking through the well-worn gear, more out of curiosity than avarice.

"Rufus holds on to our winnings for us," Heraklia explained. "Otherwise we might just spend it on something frivolous—like our freedom. Isn't that right, Rufus?"

But the lanista was too distracted to hear the jibe, trying to listen through a gap in the stable's slat wall to the goings-on inside.

Myrine pulled a small white object from the pile. "What's this?"

That drew Rufus's attention. "Something valuable?"

Before he could snatch it up, Heraklia took possession of the item: a thin bone hairpin with a tiny carving of a woman's head and shoulders as its finial. "It is a token of our goddess. Agave was the one who brought us to her. I know who should have this."

Rufus was about to protest when their distinguished visitor emerged from the stable. "That was quick," he observed, but lost his leer when he caught sight of the dark expression on the man's face. As he stormed out of the yard, Rufus scurried after him, yelling out apologies for any and all offense.

Camilla watched them go from the doorway. When Heraklia handed her the bone pin, she would not meet the older woman's eyes.

"So, you're still here."

"Where was I supposed to go?"

Heraklia nodded in the direction Camilla's father had just exited.

"What, and give up show business?!" Camilla joked bitterly. She had long ago abandoned any fantasies of that man riding to her rescue. "He'd only lock me away on some country estate where I couldn't be an embarrassment to him anymore. That is, until the foreman decided he could promote himself by knocking up the master's daughter."

"Have this all worked out, do you?"

Rufus reappeared in the yard, mopping his brow, and addressed his small company, "It took some brilliant negotiating on my part, but I think I've saved the day. We're to do an encore . . . gratis." He almost choked on that last word. "Tonight, we'll be doing Boudica."

"You're kidding!" This was too much for Camilla to keep silent. "Will we be doing Spartacus next?!"

Rufus laid her flat with a single backhanded blow. It was easy to forget, underneath the paunch, he had once had a promising career as a fighter. But that was before he lost the arm.

"You are in enough trouble already!" He growled and turned to the others, "Lots to do, people. We need spears, swords, something that'll pass for soldiers' helmets. I saw an old two-wheeled cart inside, that'll have to do for a chariot." Indicating Heraklia, "You, you'll play Boudica."

"No," Camilla said, struggling to her feet. "Let me. I know how to drive a chariot."

"You're too small. Besides, the customer requested her special."

Suddenly, all became clear to Camilla, but before she could raise another objection, Heraklia stepped between them.

Rufus clasped the woman by the shoulders. "Do this for me," he declared, in a voice loud enough for all to hear, "and you'll have your freedom."

Where there had been a frenzy of activity, there was now dead silence. This was not an offer Rufus made lightly, or ever.

Heraklia considered him for a long moment. Something unspoken passed between the two veterans. "All right," she said finally, "but we will need to prepare our souls." It was an outlandish request, but she knew desperation when she saw it. "There's a temple not far. We would be back in plenty of time."

Rufus was taken aback but could not argue. "Just there and back, no side trips. And, of course, you'll have an escort."

"Of course."

5

BLOOD SPORT

On the blood-soaked floor of the packed amphitheater, two hulking gladiators exchange deadly blows as the crowd screams and goads them on. One warrior falls, and while his adversary stands poised, makes a desperate plea to the audience for mercy. He is met with jeers and turned thumbs, spelling his doom. The image is powerful and pervasive, and one that has gone far in shaping popular perceptions of Romans as cruel and dissipate. Yet, the Western world continues to venerate this ancient civilization, regarding it—rightly or wrongly—as an illustrious ancestor, and finding in it much to admire and emulate. These two seemingly conflicting views have long maintained an uneasy coexistence.

Taking their cues from their counterparts in antiquity, generations of academics had been satisfied to dismiss the less palatable aspects of classical societies. Gladiatorial contests, animal hunts, and mass public executions were the aberrant diversions of the uncultured masses: one half of the "bread and circuses" (*panem et circenses*)—to use a phrase coined by Juvenal—that kept the rabble quiescent and dulled their ambition.[1] These were sentiments echoed by the intellectuals of the age, including Tacitus and Seneca, and reinforced by imperial biographers, such as Suetonius, who characterized only the most twisted and debauched of emperors as reveling unduly in such proceedings. Upon closer examination, however, it would seem that the sources for these characterizations, the literary elite of the day, like their imperial leaders and Roman society as a whole, had a much more complex relationship with the events of the arena than previously supposed.

It is, in fact, impossible to separate the Romans' legendary appetite for spectacle from their sober orators, enduring architecture, and military might. For a people who prided themselves on a citizenry of commanding and austere soldier-farmers and their demure and levelheaded wives, it might appear the ultimate in contradiction that innumerable idle hours were spent in the stands of the amphitheater, theater, and circus, but it is in this very contradiction that modern scholars hope to gain an insight into the Roman mind-set and mores.

Historian Michael Grant, writing in the 1960s, struggled to reconcile the Romans' lasting contributions to civilization with the perverse pleasure they took in watching two human beings fight to the death.[2] To him, this penchant for depravity classed them among the perpetrators of some of the worst human atrocities of all time: brutality on a scale that would not see its equal until the modern era. He did, however, defend the exploration of this fundamental paradox as integral to understanding the psychology and society of these empire builders. Since then, a substantial body of literature has developed on the subject.

With its genesis in early funerary practices, gladiatorial combat was not a part of the Roman games as originally conceived. The games themselves, or *ludi*, began as religious celebrations held in tribute to one or another of the myriad gods of the Roman pantheon.[3] These were festival days, holidays sanctioned and bankrolled by the state with entertainments organized by government officials. Initially, most of the action took place within the circus, an enormous elliptical racetrack. Events included animal hunts (*venationes*) and athletic competitions such as footraces, boxing, and wrestling. Chariot races were a particular crowd favorite, with successful charioteers able to achieve fame and wealth on par with that enjoyed by top gladiators. Special dramatic performances, also a prominent feature of the days' events, were mounted in theaters or other venues sacred to the deity. The earliest recorded public games were held in Rome in the fourth century B.C. There is no mention of gladiators at this time, and purpose-built amphitheaters for such displays were still centuries away. How mortal combat came to be the centerpiece of later games is a matter of considerable debate.

By the time the Romans began their meteoric rise to power in the mid–first millennium B.C., human sacrifice would have been seen as a time-honored part of the funerary rites of cultures past. They could, for example, read of Patroclus's funeral in the *Iliad* when the noble Achilles put twelve Trojan prisoners of war to the sword and threw their bodies on the pyre alongside offerings of horses, hunting dogs, and jars of precious oil and honey.[4] The practice was such an accepted part of ancient traditions that, in the first-century-B.C. *Aeneid*, Virgil's Trojan hero Aeneas sends the body of his comrade, Pallas, back to his Greek homeland for proper burial along with spoils of war and bound prisoners, "the blood of whose slaying was to sprinkle the flames."[5]

Such sacrifices were not simply the stuff of epic literature, however. In addition to tales of the Amazons, Herodotus returned from his journeys with a detailed account of how the barbaric Scythians marked the deaths of their kings. After touring the length and breadth of the countryside with the monarch's carefully prepared and preserved body, a retinue of followers laid him to rest in a large earthen mound. The late ruler was accompanied by one of his concubines, who had been specially strangled for the occasion, as well as many others, similarly dispatched, to see to the king's every need in the afterlife. These attendants included a cook, a courier, and a groom to care for the numerous horses that were also slaughtered. A year later, mourners would revisit the burial site and fifty more royal servants and retainers would be killed, stuffed, and mounted on an equal number of sacrificed horses to stand perpetual guard around the king's mound.[6]

It had long been thought that the Etruscans, too, followed the custom of shedding blood to honor the dead. Indeed, first-century-B.C. historian Nikolaos of Damascus laid the inspiration for Roman gladiatorial games squarely at their feet.[7] Recently, however, scholars have begun to question the accuracy of this attribution. The Etruscan people once dominated the lands north of the Tiber, including what is now modern Tuscany and parts of Umbria. There is little doubt these neighbors to the north had a tremendous influence on the early development of Rome. In the sixth century B.C., the last men to rule over Rome as kings were of Etruscan extraction, and even after republic took the place of monarchy, they continued to be perceived as powerful rivals. Etruscan autonomy was among the first casualties of Roman expansion when, over the course of the next few centuries, the once undistinguished city-state extended its dominion to encompass the whole of the Italian peninsula.

Brilliantly colored paintings cover the walls of the Etruscans' rock-cut tombs. Among the scenes depicted are a wide variety of athletic competitions that attest to a possible Etruscan link to games as an element in funeral ceremonies. Animal hunts are also represented—another mainstay of the fare later available in the amphitheater—as are parades or dances that include armed men, but only one rare figure seems to truly foreshadow the human carnage to come. The "Phersu," masked and bearded men with the conical caps, appear to have been specialist dog handlers.[8] Representations of these enigmatic figures have been found in just three tombs from the Etruscan necropolis at Tarquinia, dating from the mid– to late sixth century B.C. They are shown holding the long winding lead of a hound as it viciously attacks a hooded man. The victim, bleeding from his many wounds tries to fend off the animal with a club. This scene could be a precursor of the hopeless mismatches between man and beast that would occur in the Roman arena, when poorly armed or even bound prisoners and criminals were set upon by wild animals as part of the midday entertainment. These are, however, the only Etruscan images amongst the depictions of races and sporting events where it is apparent the intended outcome is the death of a man. We must look elsewhere for evidence of armed duels as a form of religious rite.

Some scholars offer up the Campanian region, south of Rome, as an alternative birthplace for the gladiator. Tomb paintings from this area dating to the latter half of the fourth century B.C. depict pairs of men locked in combat with shields and long swords or lances.[9] This is no mock battle, as they bleed copiously from gashes on their bared legs and chests, but neither do they appear to be engaged in actual warfare. Occasionally, another character in a dignified robe and long beard appears at the edge of the scene, seeming to preside over the fight, perhaps as a judge. Other tableaus in the same tombs include boxing matches and chariot races, interpreted to be funereal games, their juxtaposition implying some connection with the dueling figures.

There is no question that Campania had a long association with gladiators. Livy mentions their having outfitted the fighters that performed at their banquets with captured weapons and armor following the Second Samnite War of the late fourth century B.C. Centuries later, some of the earliest recorded and most prestigious gladiator schools were located in this territory, particularly in and around the town of Capua, where Julius Caesar himself is said to have established a *ludus*.[10] The region continued to maintain its reputation and bragging rights as a source for fighting talent throughout the Roman period.[11]

Historian Alison Futrell, however, rejects the notion of Campania as the original source of transmission, arguing that Roman views toward the area's uncouth and fractious inhabitants made it doubtful they would have found anything there worth imitating.[12] She points instead to the influential Etruscans as a far more likely candidate for dissemination if, in fact, the ancient authors are to be taken at their word that this practice ever was a foreign introduction. The possibility exists that this explanation may have simply been a pretense so oft repeated as to become accepted by those who found it difficult to reconcile such barbaric displays with a society that claimed to have advanced beyond the need for human sacrifice. Despite repeated assertions to the contrary, the ritual slaughter of humans may not have been quite so alien to the Romans as they made it out to be. Three times during the late third and second centuries B.C. the Senate, in consultation with the prophetic Sibylline books, ordered a rite in which a Gallic couple and a Greek couple were buried alive in the Forum Boarium, a public market once used for the sale of cattle. The same governing body also felt it necessary to enact an express ban on the taking of a human life in the context of magical rites and ritual cannibalism as late as 97 B.C.[13]

The need for bloodshed to propitiate the spirits of the restless dead was, however, retained in the Roman notion of the gladiatorial games as *munera*, services rendered as a duty or a tribute to the deceased. Powerful Romans would leave express instructions in their wills for contests to be held in their honor and it was the responsibility, or *munus*, of their heirs to see these wishes carried out. The stipulations of these last testaments could be extremely detailed, specifying the number and types of duels to be staged. In one such document, attractive female combatants were requested.[14]

Early *munera* consisted of no more than a few modest pairs of gladiators fighting to the death at the prominent Roman's graveside or in some other large open area, but by the end of the third century B.C., these displays had begun to escalate steadily in both scale and duration. It is traditionally held that Romans witnessed their first gladiator show in 264 B.C. when, to mark his father's passing, the son of Junius Brutus Pera held a contest between three pairs of men in the Forum Boarium. By the time of the funeral of Marcus Aemilius Lepidus in 216 B.C., the numbers had risen to twenty-two pairs.

Seventy-four gladiators performed in 174 B.C. at Titus Flaminius's games on the occasion of the death of his father, with combat taking place over a three-day period.[15]

For centuries, obligations to the dead continued to be the pretext behind these gruesome yet extremely popular exhibitions, but they also served ancillary social and political functions that eventually eclipsed their original religious intent. Like the financing of public works, the provision of mass entertainment was another way in which influential families could demonstrate their prestige and political hopefuls could curry favor with constituents. While the supervision of *ludi* in conjunction with religious celebrations similarly afforded an individual the opportunity for self-promotion, these events were seen as a duty of a sitting magistrate, usually an aedile, who was charged with the oversight of public works as well as festivals, and were subsidized out of the state coffers. The presiding official might choose to supplement the monies officially allocated with his own personal resources in order to ensure a suitably impressive show, but this was a matter of choice. By contrast, early *munera* were entirely privately funded and sponsorship was not tied to any particular office.

The costs involved in mounting a *munus*, however, could be exorbitant and represented a considerable financial burden for the heirs. It was therefore permissible to postpone such events for months, even years, until sufficient funds could be raised. Over time it became apparent that some canny individuals were intentionally withholding their right to hold a *munus* until politically opportune moments, such as during their candidacy for high office.

Soon, ambitious politicos of every stripe were finding reasons to hold greater and more elaborate *munera* in the hopes of gaining popularity and advancing their careers. Julius Caesar himself won great acclaim for the sensational games he arranged as he worked his way up the ladder of power. His own father was some twenty years gone before the conditions of his will were fulfilled by his son and heir, as Caesar left the prospect of unmatched entertainments dangling in front of a salivating electorate. According to the biographer Suetonius, once Caesar secured the office of aedile in 65 B.C., the magnitude of the display he proposed to honor his late father so alarmed his rivals that a law was rushed through the Senate limiting the number of gladiators that an individual might keep in Rome. Even still, the reduced event was said to include over three hundred pairs of fighters. Caesar, like so many up-and-comers, went into terrific debt in order to provide these games, borrowing against his lucrative future in politics. For him, at least, it was a gamble that soon paid off when, in 61 B.C., he was appointed governor of Spain. Provincial governors were infamous for making the most of their time abroad and bleeding the locals dry with demands of taxes and tribute. Caesar appears to have been little different, for in less than two years he had enough to pay off his creditors and then some.[16]

Caesar was also the first to hold funerary games for a woman, following the death of his daughter Julia, and took full advantage of the custom of providing games as part of the celebration of a military triumph. Triumphal games straddled the line between *munera* and *ludi*. Awarded by a vote of the Senate, a triumph was the highest of military accolades. Victorious generals were allowed to enter Rome in elaborate processions, parading their captured spoils through the streets for all to see. In a show of thanks to the gods for his safe return, an individual so honored also had the right to hold "votive games." These exhibitions often included gladiatorial contests and, although piety was the professed motivation, did much to enhance the reputation of the sponsor, for it was the general himself, not the state, who was expected to foot all the bills.

Some scholars suggest a significant split with tradition occurred at the end of the second century B.C. when magistrates began to mount gladiatorial contests in an official capacity. If so, this would indicate a breakdown of the formal distinctions between *munera* and *ludi*. Although both involved large public gatherings, a *munus* was ultimately a private matter and, as such, provided a venue for personal aggrandizement, while *ludi* were intended as communal offerings to the gods by the populace as a whole, despite being organized and sometimes even partially funded by an individual in his capacity as representative of the state. Historian Thomas Wiedemann attributes this confusion between the public roles of politicians and their acts as private citizens to the people's expectation that aediles and praetors, as lower-level worthies on the fast track to fame and glory, would find excuses to mount *munera* during their term of service in order to further their own political aspirations.[17]

As production grew to keep pace with demand, Romans were soon made painfully aware of the dangers inherent in trying to keep scores of highly trained warriors with little left to lose under lock and key. In 73 B.C., an uprising began in Capua, the heart of Campanian gladiator country. The revolt was led by Spartacus, a name that has yet to fade from history. Although his exploits were famed throughout the ancient world, his story comes down to us from only two, somewhat divergent, accounts by Plutarch and Appian, Greek writers of the second century A.D.

Thracian by birth, Spartacus' origins are fairly murky. He was alleged to have been a shepherd, a bandit leader, even a soldier in the Roman army, before finding himself at the business end of those very same forces, as a captured criminal or enemy soldier. He was then sold into slavery and forced to become a gladiator. According to Plutarch, conditions at the training school in Capua where Spartacus was sent were particularly difficult. The trainer in charge, Lentulus Batiates, was known for his cruelty, keeping his fighters in close quarters and confined to their cells when not fighting.[18] It was not long before a plan was hatched, and Spartacus and seventy-eight of his fellows fought their way to freedom with kitchen knives and cooking spits. Rampaging across the landscape while eluding their pursuers at every turn, the group gained terrific notoriety while amassing more formidable weapons and numbers. When they set up an armed encampment in the crater of the dormant Mount Vesuvius, however, they were still considered little more than rabble and a contingent of the Roman army was dispatched to clean up this minor insurgence. In short order, Spartacus's forces dealt the Romans a series of humiliating defeats, further enhancing their legend.

Over the next two years, the disenfranchised from all over the countryside were drawn to the rebel cause by the hundreds, transforming the ragtag group into a veritable army of forty thousand strong, according to some estimates. Dissent was fomenting among the ranks as well. Flush with their many victories and the elite Roman forces put to rout, many wished to remain in southern Italy and continue their plundering ways, but Spartacus could see no good end to this and advocated leading the party farther north, perhaps to escape Italy altogether and return home. He and his followers made great progress toward this goal, clashing at Picenum in central Italy with four Roman legions. Despite having been personally led by Rome's two sitting consuls, the city's ruling magistrates, Spartacus' forces won out against the renowned Roman military machine and continued on. The Roman governor of Cisalpine Gaul, the province of northern Italy, was next to be defeated, but just as the Alps were within reach, Spartacus deviated south again for some unknown reason. There, they met up against the troops of Licinius Crassus, a shrewd politician and businessman, who eventually ran Spartacus and his depleted forces to ground. To dissuade any who might consider following in his footsteps, six thousand of Spartacus' men were crucified along the main road between Capua and Rome.

Following the Spartacan Revolt, the Roman government became increasingly wary of individuals who might accumulate large gladiator troupes, fearing their use as personal armies. This was of particular concern during the Catilinarian Conspiracy of 63 B.C., prompting the Senate to send the growing number of gladiators out of Rome and disperse them among schools in other towns. These warriors figured in later conflicts as well, but more as a threat that was never really put to the test. Caesar was thought to have a great band of gladiators waiting in the wings during his play for power in the civil war of the early 40s B.C. Marc Antony, too, kept gladiators at Cyzicus in Asia Minor, hoping to use them against Octavian, the future first emperor Augustus, during their struggle to succeed Caesar after his death in 44 B.C.[19] Sometime during the Principate, it became expressly forbidden for private citizens to keep their own gladiators in Rome. Only the troupes owned by the emperor himself were allowed.

The distinction between private and state occasions became even more blurred in the power and the person of the emperor, as he became the primary sponsor of games in Rome. Each successive ruler jealously guarded the right to hold any type of mass entertainment in the city, wary that those who would challenge their right to rule might use them to sway public sentiment. From the reign of Augustus onward, increasing restrictions were placed on who could sponsor games, how long they would last and how many participants they could have. By the reign of Domitian at the end of the first century A.D., it was not longer permitted for anyone besides the emperor himself to hold games in Rome, unless a member of the imperial family or an official representative, such as a praetor, organizing them in the emperor's name. The emperor also reserved the right to celebrate military triumphs, as he was now the de facto head of the army and all campaigns were waged on his behalf.

Elsewhere in Italy and the provinces, it was still possible for private citizens to stage *munera*. A *Satyricon* banqueter eagerly anticipates such an event:

> Our Titus is a generous sort, and an aficionado. You can say what you like, it's going to be a big deal. I'm a friend of his, and I can tell you he doesn't do things halfway. He'll put on the best swords, no running away, with a pile of bodies in the middle for the whole audience to see. He has the wherewithal to do it too. He inherited 30 million sesterces from his father who died prematurely. So if he spends 400,000 he doesn't feel the pinch at all.[20]

Well in advance of the date, an *editor* would be sure to advertise impending games—large or small—with posted notices (*edicta munera*) and town criers. Professionally painted signs heralding several different events were found on walls along the main thoroughfares of Pompeii. The shows described are of an average scale for a town of Pompeii's modest size, spanning multiple days and offering twenty to thirty pairs of gladiators all told. Announcements followed a general pattern that conveyed all salient facts of interest to the public: how long the entertainment would last, how many fighters were to be exhibited, what schools they were from or to whom they belonged, and most important, who the people had to thank for this munificence and the occasion for which the show was being held. Any special attractions were also noted, such as wild animal hunts, featured performers, or the use of awnings to shade spectators from the afternoon sun.

Fight fans had a number of opportunities to inspect the competitors up close before seeing them in action on the arena floor. A day or so before their scheduled appearance, participants would be formally presented in some public area, such as the town forum. This was a good way to become familiar with new blood at the local *ludus* and take the measure of visiting teams. In those towns with permanently established schools, gladiators could also be observed in practice, although those allowed within the walls of the school were probably the most privileged, there by invitation of the owner. On the eve of the games, however, a feast was often held for the contestants that was open to all and sundry.

The official commencement of festivities began the next day with a parade, or *pompa*. The sponsor of the games presided over the procession that wended its way to and through the amphitheater to the blare of trumpets. He was accompanied by attendants bearing symbols of his rank and images of the gods of the Roman state. Religious belief permeated every act in the ritually charged atmosphere of the arena and a number of deities were seen to have especially close ties to this world. Mars, the god of war, and Hercules, the divine hero, were favorites among the soldiery and their martial qualities translated well to the amphitheater. The goddess Victory was also one to be courted for her awards of palm fronds and laurel wreathes, but it was Nemesis, goddess of destiny, retribution, and changeable fortune, who seems to have held particular sway over events as they were to unfold. Shrines in honor of this lesser known deity have been found built into many amphitheaters throughout the empire. Some of these chapels of Nemesis, or *nemesea*, could be accessed from the sponsor's box as well as from the arena itself, suggesting that both *editor* and gladiator had reason to entreat the goddess for a favorable outcome to their risky endeavors.[21]

The day's participants also marched in the *pompa*. Their ornate arms and armor were not worn in the procession, but borne alongside on large litters or in the hands of attendants, as portrayed on a Pompeian tomb relief now in the Naples Museum. Most of the helmets and gladiatorial gear unearthed at Pompeii were so elaborate it was initially believed they could only have been intended for parade purposes. Marcus Junkelmann, however, contests this theory. Having himself staged experiments with replicas of the Pompeii pieces, he argues these forms would have withstood considerable battering despite their embellishments, and are completely in keeping with depictions of equipment in use at the time.[22] It would be a fallacy to assume that Romans would have been any less willing to sacrifice costly paraphernalia than they were the human beings who wore them.

As a lasting symbol of the grandeur and excess of ancient Rome, the Colosseum was a relatively late addition to the capital's cityscape. Ten years in the making, this architectural marvel was not finished until A.D. 80. Only much later, during the medieval period, did it receive its famous moniker: a reference, not to its own massive size, but to its proximity to a colossal statue of the emperor Nero that once stood nearby. It is more accurately termed the Flavian Amphitheater, after the reigning dynasty founded by T. Flavius Vespasianus (the emperor Vespasian) who ordered its construction, and his sons, Titus and Domitian, who succeeded him and saw the structure to its completion.

Prior to the creation of a permanent home for the games, exhibitions were staged in other ready venues, such as theaters and the immense Circus Maximus, which could accommodate an estimated two hundred thousand or more spectators. Temporary timber stands were also assembled in large public spaces around the city, such as the Forum Boarium and the military parade ground, the Campus Martius. Because of the dangers inherent in displays of armed combatants and wild animals, purpose-built structures came to be preferred. With seating raised well above the floor of an enclosed arena, it was the wooden elliptical installation in Rome's main forum, the Forum Romanum, which is thought to have provided the prototype for the amphitheaters to follow.[23]

Although derived from the Greek, meaning "with views from both sides," the amphitheater was a distinctly Roman innovation. Its overall plan has not changed much over the millennia and would be recognizable to any modern sports fan. The first recorded amphitheater in Rome opened sometime in either 30 or 29 B.C., but Pliny the Elder mentions a rather fantastic antecedent.[24] Some twenty years earlier, an ingenious contraption had been devised by a politician named C. Scribonius Curio that was actually two buildings in one. Curio's novel (though somewhat precarious) design consisted of two semicircular theaters that could rotate on an enormous pivot. In the morning, a different show could be presented in each of the two halves while, in the afternoon, the structures could close ranks to form an amphitheater.

The earliest extant example of a stone amphitheater comes not from Rome at all; rather, it is Pompeii's arena that holds this distinction. Built around 80 B.C., its plan is primitive compared to later examples, but already it contained most of the elements typical of the form. Rows of raked benches radiated out from a central oval field, providing an unobstructed view of events below. These rows were divided into three horizontal sections, or tiers (*maeniana*). The seats of the lower tier were reserved for local dignitaries and were accessed through separate points of entry from the upper tiers, which were reached via exterior staircases. Similar to methods used in theater construction, Pompeii's arena floor was set below ground level and the excavated soil was piled up all around to form the earthen core of the stadium seating. Because of this solid foundation, it lacked the complex internal structure of later freestanding examples, particularly the Colosseum, where the seating area rose high above ground level and was honeycombed behind and below with concentric arcades, numerous exits (*vomitoria*), and stairways for easy conveyance of crowds to and from their seats.[25]

Nine years before the discovery of Great Dover Street Woman, a team from the Museum of London's Archaeological Service found what may have been the site of her final performance: the London amphitheater. Up until that time, the location of this important edifice had been unknown. What had begun as a routine excavation—this time in preparation for the construction of a new art gallery in the Corporation of London's Guildhall yard—suddenly became big news when a oddly curved masonry wall was revealed to be this missing piece of the puzzle of Roman London. Simple, with a plan comparable to the Pompeii example, this amphitheater had also a sunken arena, but had originally been built entirely of wood and was only partially revetted in stone in later centuries. Using a technique called dendrochronology, where the annual growth of tree rings are used to determine the age of a wooden object, the date for the felling of the oldest timbers in the structure came to A.D. 70, not long before the woman at Great Dover Street is thought to have met her death.

Twenty meters outside the London amphitheater's eastern entrance were found the cones of the Mediterranean stone pine (*Pinus pinea*), some still attached to branches, suggesting they had not fallen far from the tree.[26] Such cones had previously been found in other Roman period deposits in Britain, but where before it had been assumed they were imported, it now looked as though the species had, in fact, been introduced to the island. The trees may have been planted around the amphitheater to provide shade and a ready source for their fragrant cones.

The presence of stone pinecones both at the London Amphitheater and in the grave of Great Dover Street Woman provides an intriguing link between the two.

Approaches to the amphitheater would have also been lined with bars, stalls, and shops where those on their way to the show could pick up food and drink, and the occasional trinket to take home. Small clay figurines depicting the more common gladiator types seem to have been a favorite keepsake. Although it is unclear whether they were intended as toys or were simply decorative objects, many examples of these statuettes, some complete with tiny removable helmets, have been found in tombs and other sites throughout the empire.

. To enter the vast bowl of the amphitheater was to step inside a monumental model of Roman society and worldview. As part of his efforts to bring about a return to traditional values, Augustus' comprehensive social reforms even went so far as to dictate seating arrangements at public gatherings.[27] Where before the classes and sexes might have intermingled indiscriminately, spectators now filed in and took their places according to rank and status. The rows closest to the arena floor were reserved for men of the higher orders and political officials. Behind them sat the lower classes in turn. Civilians sat separate from soldiers, married men were sorted from the unmarried. Youths who had not yet taken the toga of manhood had their own section with their tutors close by, so as to mold their young minds and advise them as to how to think and react to the carnage they witnessed.

In this way, according to the biographer Suetonius, Augustus hoped to reinforce social distinctions and avoid embarrassing incidents such as when a respected senator was left standing because none would make room for him on the benches of a crowded theater. However, while it might seem that there was a place for everyone and everyone was in their place, not every person who wanted a seat was guaranteed to get one. Amphitheaters were mammoth structures, designed to accommodate an audience of thousands, sometimes tens of thousands, but this usually represented only a fraction of the local population. It is estimated that the Colosseum could hold an astonishing fifty to sixty thousand spectators, but this was in a city where popular estimates place the total inhabitants at over a million. Hardly a significant proportion compared to the London example, whose paltry six thousand seats actually represented almost a third of the town's residents. Pompeii's amphitheater is one of the few whose capacity may have been on par with its population, but many of its twenty thousand seats may have been occupied by visitors from neighboring towns with no such facilities, as well as those who dwelled on the grand estates in the surrounding countryside.

As sponsor of a show and host, the *editor* handed out the majority of tickets to friends, relatives, and political cronies. To strengthen their position as patrons, recipients passed this largesse along to their own clients in turn. In the provinces, private benefactors and corporate dues-paying organizations, known as *collegia*, who contributed to the upkeep or renovation of an amphitheater, might also control blocks of seats to allocate as they saw fit. Those without adequate social and political connections were all but shut out of this distribution process. If they could afford it, there were sometimes tickets left over that would be sold directly to the public or could be obtained (no doubt at greater expense) from a scalper (*locarius*).[28] There were also some shows arranged by nonaristocrats for which admission was charged (*munera assiforana*), but these displays likely paled in comparison to those mounted by the emperor and leading lights of the community. The *Aes Italicense* of A.D. 177 records that the maximum expenditure allowed for such games fell at the low end of the scale of those allowed for aristocrats, priests, and politicians. Emperors occasionally put on events that were open to the public free of charge, but tickets were still limited. Suetonius records that the noise made by people camped out from the wee hours to obtain free seats to the circus once so infuriated Caligula, he had them driven away with cudgels.[29] In the ensuing stampede, dozens in the crowd were killed, including several respectable matrons and more than twenty members of the noble class of knights.

Where women—in the eyes of Suetonius—had once mixed "promiscuously" with men in the stands, Augustus's legislation consigned them to the uppermost tier of the amphitheater. Early in the history of gladiatorial contests, women had been all but excluded from these bloody and violent displays. By the late first century B.C. when Augustus began his reign, the situation had changed significantly. Women had emerged from the domestic sphere to become a much more visible segment of society, attending shows in the theater, circus, and amphitheater with impunity. Augustus did not attempt to bar their presence at gladiatorial games but drew the line when it came to wrestling. In the fashion of the ancient Greeks, many athletic events were still conducted in the nude, but upstanding and proper Romans, like Cicero and Tacitus, frowned on such decadent exhibitions out of principle.[30] For women to watch two naked men grapple went well beyond the bounds of decency. Augustus was said to have delayed the appearance of a pair of acclaimed wrestlers until the next morning and sent criers around the city to announce that women should not make their way to the amphitheater on that day until the afternoon.

Although women were often banned from attending sporting events, there is evidence that some participated as professional athletes. This also seems to have been a holdover from the Greeks who allowed girls to compete publicly until they reached marriageable age. An inscription from Delphi, dating to the mid–first century A.D., commemorates the many achievements of a trio of daughters of Hermesianax of Tralles who excelled in a variety of sports.[31] One of the three, Hedea, seems particularly versatile, having won two footraces at major competitions, a chariot race run in full armor, and a kithara-singing contest that she had entered in the boys' category. In the mid–fourth century B.C., the Greek philosopher Plato recommended that girls under the age of puberty be allowed to compete in the nude while those over thirteen should wear some covering.[32] There is little mention of the proper attire for Roman female athletes, but a fourth-century-A.D. mosaic from a villa at Piazza Armerina in Sicily depicts a number of women clad in rather modern-looking bikinis. They are shown vying in activities involving balls and weights for prizes of crowns and palm fronds. A bronze statuette now in the Hamburg Museum depicts another female athlete who holds aloft a bent sword or a *strigilis*, a curved metal utensil used to scrape oil and dust off the body following exercise.[33] One knee wrapped in a brace, she is clothed only in a pair of leather briefs, secured at either hip with thong ties. A preserved example of very similar briefs was found in an excavation at Queen's Street, London.

Although the exact date of Augustus's "Theatrical Law" is not certain, Ovid ran afoul of the decorum-conscious emperor when he dared compose *The Art of Love*, parts of which read like an instruction manual on how and where to conduct an illicit affair. According to the poet, the press of bodies on the crowded benches of the circus was especially well suited for flirting between lovers, provided they could sit together. Augustus put an end to the possibility of such assignations when he segregated women in the stands. For his impudence, he also had Ovid exiled to a backwater town along the Black Sea in A.D. 8.

The only women permitted to have a view from ringside were the six priestesses of the goddess Vesta, know as the Vestal Virgins. Theirs was a situation unique among women in Roman society. Entering the service of their deity between the ages of six and ten, they vowed to remain chaste and incorruptible keepers of the sacred hearth of Rome for the next thirty years. The power and respect their office commanded was reflected in the place of honor reserved for them in the amphitheater. With the rise of Christianity, however, their unassailable position as paragons of virtue came under fire from Christian writers like Prudentius:

There she sits conspicuous with the awe-inspiring trappings of her head-bands and enjoys what the trainers have produced. What a soft, gentle heart! She rises at the blows, and every time a victor stabs his victim's throat she calls him her pet.[34]

The Vestals commanded some of the best seats in the house, at one end of the short axis of the elliptical arena, opposite the "praetor's tribunal," the box for the sponsor of the games and his entourage.[35] The imperial box (*pulvinar*) was located nearby on this same level and other women of influence, such as members of the emperor's family, would occasionally sit among the Vestals as their guests. Along with the emperor, the presiding magistrate, and the Vestal Virgins, the seats up front were occupied by senators and other notables. Collectively known as the *podium* level, these rows were set above the sheer arena wall, which could be several meters high in order to protect the spectators from the dangerous activities below. Often concern that even this insurmountable palisade would be insufficient to ward off flung weapons and leaping carnivores prompted some to be augmented with iron grilles or nets strung between posts. The *podium* itself was usually ornately decorated with marble and mosaics, and was wider than the rows behind so as to accommodate more comfortable chairs, which the VIPs brought for themselves.[36]

But as these dignitaries had a clear view of everything, so too were they in full sight of everyone, and none more so than the emperor himself. In the microcosm of the amphitheater, where Roman concepts of justice and power were played out to gory effect, the role of the emperor was especially complicated and intriguing. Like those struggling for survival on the floor of the amphitheater floor, so too was the Roman ruler on display in his special box in the stands. This was the closest most subjects would ever get to his vaunted personage, and they took the opportunity to scrutinize his every gesture and mood. An emperor was expected to be the Roman citizen par excellence, the supreme *paterfamilias*, yet the reality often fell short of the mark. Detractors were quick to pounce on any perceived flaw.

In the ancient literature, some emperors drew criticism for not holding enough games during their reign or not appearing to enjoy the ones they did hold enough. Tiberius won no love from the people for organizing no games of his own and setting limits on the size of the *munera* others might present.[37] Augustus, Tiberius' stepfather and predecessor, had been a tough act to follow. In Augustus' *Res gestae*, the first emperor gives a personal accounting of the numerous athletic competitions, animal hunts, and state games he held during his reign, including eight grand spectacles provided in his own name and that of his sons and grandsons in which ten thousand men were said to have fought. He also mounted an enormous naval battle (*naumachia*) on a man-made lake in which three thousand men did battle.[38] Tiberius made no attempt to match these efforts and kept the strings of the public purse taut.

An even greater transgression than appearing too stingy with the mass entertainments was to show too much enthusiasm for them. Several emperors were demonized for getting carried away by "gladiator mania." In their youths, some more moderate rulers, such as Hadrian and Titus, were said to have trained in gladiatorial techniques, either tempted by the romance of the arena or driven by a more practical need for weapons skills, but it was only the worst of the worst who were characterized as harboring an unhealthy obsession with public performance.[39] To ancient historians, the willingness of these so-called "bad" emperors to overstep the bounds of propriety and indulge their slightest whim was both symbol and symptom of a debauched nature.

Among the most infamous, Nero's passion for the stage is well-known, while a great deal was made of both Caligula's and Commodus' antics in the amphitheater. Caligula trained as a *thraex* and maintained his own personal *ludus*, but Pliny the Elder found the fighters to be of uneven quality: Only two of the thousands housed there would not blink when threatened.[40] A staunch supporter of his Thracian brothers in arms, Caligula was once said to have poured poison in the wounds of a fighter simply because he was a *murmillo*, enemy of the *thraeces*.[41] Commodus, too, fancied himself a gladiator; he also fancied himself the god Hercules, but that is another story. Although he professed to be trained in all weaponry, in the amphitheater he would cut down hundreds of exotic animals—tigers, hippopotami, and elephants among these—with a bow from a safe distance.[42] He was also said to have dispatched numerous ostriches in this way and fought with only wooden weapons on the arena floor, while at the same time awarding himself with an outlandish fee for his performance. Ultimately, he met his end at the hands of an athlete named Narcissus who, as part of a conspiracy between several top officials and Commodus' own concubine, strangled him while he spent the night at a gladiator school on the eve of the New Year A.D. 193.

The mass slaughter of animals was the typical start to a day's program in the amphitheater. One of the schools in Rome, the Ludus Matutinus, specialized in training hunters (*venatores*) for these events, which could consist of anything from presentations of trained or exotic creatures to the pitting of predator against prey or human against animal. *Venationes* had a separate but parallel development to the gladiatorial games themselves, allegedly arising out of the capture of elephants and other unfamiliar species when Rome clashed with Carthage on the North African coast for supremacy in the western Mediterranean during the Punic Wars from the mid–third to mid–second centuries B.C. The display and eventual massacre of animals from conquered territory, just like that of human captives, graphically symbolized Rome's growing domination over the ancient world. During the second consulship of Pompey in 55 B.C., some one thousand lions and leopards were slain before audiences at Rome, while getting their first look at such alien creatures as the northern European lynx and the Indian rhinoceros.[43]

Beasts of all shapes and sizes, drawn from every corner of the empire, would be driven into the arena through one of the entrance tunnels or, in the case of more elaborate structures, hauled up through the floor using elaborate mechanisms. At the London Amphitheater, small chambers were found flanking the eastern entrance that have been interpreted as pens where animals would await release into the arena, similar to the way bulls are introduced into the ring at a bullfight or rodeo.[44] According to Michael Fulford, an expert in the customs of the games:

> It became a greater and greater spectacle. You would try and make the performance more exciting than the last one. We have sources which describe hundreds of wild animals from Africa and Syria, from all parts of the empire, bringing in stags from Britain for example and mixing them in different combinations.

However, environmental archaeologist Jane Sidell reports that the bones of animals found at London's amphitheater tended toward the less exotic:

> The species we have include things like horses, cows, we have some pigs as well. We did have dogs and Roman Britain was well-known for the hunting dogs that were exported from Britain to the continent. So it seems likely that dogs that had been specially trained were used in the arena for these combats.

Other remains found at this site included those of a bear and numerous skulls of bulls. Both of these species, along with big cats, especially lions, tigers, and panthers, were used for even more sinister purposes during the midday events, when helpless victims were summarily executed by claws, hoofs, horns, and teeth.

Although they shared the same stage, gladiators stood at the opposite end of the spectrum from the wretched multitudes herded into the arena to meet a horrific end. Conquered enemies were sometimes massacred publicly by the hundreds, even thousands, in an all too real demonstration of Rome's dominion. Josephus, historian and eyewitness to the long and bitter Jewish War (A.D. 66–70), reports that following the fall and destruction of Jerusalem, numerous shows were held by Titus, future emperor and leader of the Roman forces in Judea, in which captive Jews perished by the scores. On just a single occasion, to mark the birthday of Titus' brother, Domitian, it is said some two thousand five hundred prisoners were immolated, forced to fight wild beasts or each other.[45]

Political dissenters and those convicted of treason met a similar fate. Among these were countless Christians, whose monotheistic beliefs were at odds with the expectation that citizens participate in the state and imperial cults. By failing to do proper homage to the gods of Rome and the deified spirits of the emperor and his family, followers of this young religion came to be eyed with distrust, as potential traitors to the empire. One of the most infamous episodes occurred after a devastating fire swept through Rome in A.D. 64. The emperor Nero found a ready-made scapegoat in the then small and powerless sect. He accused them of starting the fire in order to deflect suspicion from himself and, according to Tacitus:

> Nero had self-acknowledged Christians arrested. Then, on their information, large numbers of others were condemned—not so much for incendiarism as for their antisocial tendencies. Their deaths were made farcical. Dressed in wild animals' skins, they

were torn to pieces by dogs, or crucified, or made into torches to
be ignited after dark as substitutes for daylight.[46]

The emperor was said to have lorded over these proceedings,
some of which were held in his own gardens, as that great Roman
amphitheater, the Colosseum, had not yet been built. Although
Tacitus considered the charges against them in this case to be fabricated, he, like so many of his contemporaries, considered the Christians "notoriously depraved" adherents of a "deadly superstition,"
but even at the time the harshness of the reprisals were thought
unwarranted:

> For it was felt that they were being sacrificed to one man's brutal-
> ity rather than to the national interest.[47]

Christians thereafter were repeatedly singled out for state-
sanctioned persecution until the fourth century A.D., when the
emperor Constantine himself converted and declared Christianity
the official religion.

The execution of criminals (*noxii*) before large numbers of
spectators was less a deterrent for future offenders than a symbolic
reinforcement of Roman ideals of justice and morality. Rome had
no facilities for long-term incarceration. Misdemeanors by members of the lower classes might lead to a period of hard labor on a
public works project, while the gentry were assessed fines or, in the
case of more serious offenses, faced the confiscation of property and
exile to an island in the Mediterranean or beyond the civilized limits of the empire. However, whether of high birth or low, certain
crimes were seen to be so heinous as to merit capital punishment.

Romans had a number of ingenious methods for carrying out a death penalty besides those involving the amphitheater. Ancient laws against parricide, the killing of a parent or grandparent, prescribed that the condemned be sewn into a sack (sometimes along with a variety of animals, including a dog, a rooster, and a snake) and cast into a river or the sea. Traitors and murderers could look forward to being hurled from the Tarpeian Rock, a high precipice in Rome named after the treacherous Tarpeia who betrayed the Roman defenders to the invading Sabines only to meet her own end at their hands.[48]

Faced with the prospect of a shameful death, some aristocrats opted for suicide. Taking one's own life was considered a far nobler act than allowing it to be taken in a disgraceful manner. Followers of Stoic philosophy, in particular, believed there was little point in struggling against destiny: If a man's death be fated, better that he should own it. In this way, Seneca the Younger found something to admire even in the deaths of two men of humble birth. When condemned to the arena, they chose to escape the torture and rob the audience of their entertainment through horrible, if resourceful, means. One choked himself in a latrine with a sponge on a stick that Romans used in lieu of toilet paper, while the other thrust his head through the spokes of the cart that was transporting him to the amphitheater.[49] These were the lengths to which some would go to avoid the torment and humiliation of the games.

Seneca had witnessed firsthand what these men were willing to take their own lives to avoid. Having once made the mistake of arriving at the amphitheater in the middle of the day, he was horrified by what he saw: men without any means of defense made to kill one another in turn, with no quarter hoped for or given. "The morning matches had been merciful by comparison," he writes. "Now all niceties were put aside, and it was pure and simple murder."[50]

The Romans, however, were capable of even more horrific acts, occasionally indulging in the ancient equivalent of "snuff films." These were reenactments of stories from mythology in which the performers would all come to messy ends. One scenario had Orpheus' lyre proving insufficient to soothe the savage beast, allowing its poor player to be torn apart by a bare.[51] The fate of the quintessential evil stepmother, Dirce, was also played out to great effect. After treating her husband's first wife, Antiope, no better than a slave, Antiope's twin sons exacted a terrible revenge on Dirce, tying her to the horns of an enraged bull. The story seems to have appealed to Roman ideas of retribution, appearing repeatedly in wall paintings in Pompeian homes and as the subject of a larger-than-life marble sculpture group now housed in the Naples Museum. In his biography of Nero, Suetonius also makes reference to a woman hidden in a wooden cow, who was mated with a bull.[52] This passage is interpreted by Kathleen Coleman as:

> A female prisoner was used in a mythological setting as the equiv-
> alent of Persiphae who fell in love with the bull on the island of
> Crete and actually mated with it. Clearly, if this was performed in
> the arena no woman would survive a congress of that nature, but
> then if she was a prisoner she wasn't meant to survive.

By the time the gladiators took the stage in the afternoon, their brand of carnage—with its weapons, armor, and rules of engagement—would have seemed refined and civilized by comparison. The barely trained novice might have had a very different perspective, however:

And now the day arrived. Now the people had assembled for the spectacle of our suffering. Now the bodies of those about to die had been put on display throughout the arena and led along in a parade of their own death. The sponsor of the event, winning favor with our blood, took his seat. Although no one could know my real status or my family or my father, from whom I was separated by the ocean, one thing nevertheless made me pitiable in the eyes of some spectator—the fact that I seemed to be unfairly matched. For I was chosen to be the designated sacrificial victim of the arena, and no one had ever been of less value to a sponsor. On all sides, everything growled with the preparation for death. One man was sharpening a sword, another was heating up metal strips in the fire. Over here, rods for flogging were being brought in, over there, whips. The trumpets began to sound with a deadly fanfare. Even before our deaths, the coffins were brought in and the funeral procession began. Everywhere there were wounds, moans, and blood.[53]

The above text is a fiction, intended to provide background for a rhetorical exercise used by students of the period to practice their oratory techniques, but it does present an evocative first-person account of the terror likely felt when entering the arena.

Gladiators made their entrance to the musical accompaniment of horns and *hydraulis*, an organ powered by water and air under pressure. These instruments are depicted in a second-century-A.D. mosaic floor from the villa at Zliten, now in the Tripoli Archaeological Museum. The musicians play along the sidelines of a frieze that depicts in great detail scenes of both *damnatio ad bestias* and gladiatorial combat.

Waiting in the wings alongside the orchestra in the mosaic is the "couch of Libitina," a wheeled stretcher used to convey the dead out of the arena. By contrast, the bodies of criminals were simply dragged from the field using ropes with hooks and draught animals, but all were headed toward the same exit: the Porta Libitinaria.[54] Named after the goddess of funerals, Libitina, this gate stood opposite the one through which the fighters entered, symbolically rendering the arena a space caught between the two worlds of life and death. All the while the gladiators fought, their fates hung in the balance, undetermined until they returned to the outside world through one or the other of the two gates.

Their performances rife with ritual and symbolism, the gladiators would go through all the proper motions in turn. Having had their weapons verified as sharp and deadly by the *editor* in the *probatio armorum* ceremony, they now turned to salute him in his box in the stands. Contrary to popular belief, and every Hollywood gladiator film, the famous phrase "Hail Caesar! We who are about to die salute you!" was an unlikely utterance on this occasion. Although the saying appears in the writings of two separate authors, Suetonius and Dio Cassius, both are describing the same event: a *naumachia* held by the emperor Claudius on the Fucine Lake. This was a mock naval battle, not a gladiatorial contest in an amphitheater, and the contestants were probably not even professional fighters, but rather prisoners doomed to a watery grave. It seems even more improbable that this expression would have caught on later considering how the original incident played out. Having been wished good health by the prisoners, Claudius returned the sentiments, but what had been intended as a rather callous joke (since none were expected to survive), was taken by the desperate men to mean the emperor had changed his mind and no longer wished them to fight. They immediately threw down their weapons, and only after much cajoling and threats did the show finally go on as planned.

As a prelude to the main event meant to whet the appetite of the audience, the gladiators might first showcase their skills by sparring with wooden weapons the same as those used in training back at the *ludus*. Soon, however, the real fighting would begin. Pairings would have been chosen by lot beforehand with careful attention paid to the proper combinations of gladiator types.

Fans cheered for their preferred category of fighter, either "big shield" (scutarii) or "small shield" (parmularii). Sometimes rivalries between factions could get out of hand and boil over in the stands, as was the case in A.D. 59, described here by Tacitus:

> There was a serious fight between the inhabitants of two Roman settlements, Nuceria and Pompeii. It arose out of a trifling incident at a gladiatorial show given by Livineius Regulus. . . . During an exchange of taunts—characteristic of these disorderly country towns—abuse led to stone-throwing, and then swords were drawn. The people of Pompeii, where the show was held, came off best. Many wounded and mutilated Nucerians were taken to the capital. Many bereavements, too, were suffered by parents and children.[55]

A wall painting from Pompeii, now in the Naples Museum, provides a bird's-eye view of this deadly clash between hometown and visitor. Fights are shown breaking out on the arena floor and in the stands under the amphitheater's unfurled awning. Combatants spill out onto the surrounding tree-lined streets, brandishing weapons as they chase one another around souvenir stalls and between buildings.

It is believed this conflict was really the culmination of some long-standing feud between the two neighboring towns that came to be inflamed by the high emotions of the games. Nevertheless, when Nero caught wind of what had occurred, he vowed to deprive the Pompeians of their precious amphitheater for no less than ten years.

Bloodshed was best kept to the floor of the arena where sand was spread thick to soak up the excess. The word *arena* was, in fact, derived from the Latin word for sand, *harena*. On this stage, gladiators put all their hard work and training to the test. A pair of referees (the *summa rudis* and his assistant, the *secunda rudis*) would officiate over each duel. The audience would be enrapt, shouting out encouragement and crying *"Habet, hoc habet!"* ("Got him! Let him have it!") when a blow connected and they thought the recipient was finished.

Once a contestant had fallen or decided he could fight no longer, he would either drop his weapon or shield, or signal his defeat by raising the forefinger of his left hand. The referee would then halt the action and look to the *editor* for a ruling. Although the fighter's fate ultimately rested with the sponsor of the games, the audience was extremely vocal about their opinions. If they thought the vanquished gladiator had displayed great valor, they would call for his life to be spared with the words *"Mitte!"* ("Let him go!") and vigorously wave the hems of their cloaks and togas.[56] Alternatively, if they were unimpressed, there would be catcalls and "turned thumbs" (*pollice verso*). The exact meaning of *pollice verso* is a matter of some debate. The term appears in the writings of Juvenal and

Prudentius, but the form this gesture took is unclear. Rather than pointing downward, the sign for death may have involved turning the thumb upward or toward the heart, imitating a sword's thrust. When death was indicated, it was for the victor to dispatch his foe. The loser, for his part, was expected to die with dignity, kneeling before his executioner and not flinching from the descending blade.

Once a gladiator had succumbed, a slave would enter the arena, dressed as the Etruscan-inspired death-demon Charon and carrying a hammer, an attribute of that deity. He would be accompanied by another figure, that of Hermes Psycopomp, who wielded a red-hot poker in the shape of a caduceus.[57] This role might also be played by a member of the arena staff in the costume of Hermes' Roman counterpart, Mercury, in his aspect as the escort of souls. If the brand applied to the body elicited no response, the fighter was determined to be beyond all feeling and the Charon character would guarantee the verdict with a blow from his hammer.

For those lucky contestants who fought and lived, their achievement could be rewarded in a variety of ways. Most commonly, a palm frond (*palma*) would be presented to the champion by the *editor*, which the fighter would then wave while running a victory lap around the arena. Such a scene is depicted in graffito from Pompeii, although its accompanying inscription shows it to be a jibe at those involved in the amphitheater riot of A.D. 59, stating that neither side had much reason to celebrate on that day. Other gifts were also given out, including purses of money (*praemium*), their sums determinded by the relative standing of the gladiator, as laid out in documents such as the *Aes Italicense*.

An outstanding performance might garner a gladiator a crown (*corona*) of laurel leaves, but only the truly rare and exceptional received the kind of popular acclaim necessary to be granted their freedom on the spot. Emancipation was signified by the conferring of a wooden sword, the *rudis*, which absolved the holder of any further obligation to fight. This very special gift was not without its price, however. While nominally bestowed by the *editor* of the games, it was usually at the urging of the crowd, but it was the event's sponsor who had to reimburse the gladiator's owner for his lost source of income.[58] The more popular the fighter, the more costly they were to manumit. This privilege and its penalty often fell to the emperor as *editor* and many rankled at having to do the people's bidding at their personal expense. Hadrian was said to have admonished the clamoring crowd, saying it was not for them to tell him to set free another man's property.[59]

Those who survived the day exited the stadium through the Porta Sanavivaria, the "Gate of Life." The less fortunate took a different path. What ultimately happened to the body of a fallen gladiator after it was removed from the arena was a matter for the deceased's comrades to decide. If the fighter had been a prisoner or slave in life, it was quite possible they would have no one to look after them in death. These unfortunates would be interred in a potter's field or simply discarded beyond the walls of the amphitheater, as may have been the case for one poor soul found by archaeologists buried just outside the London Amphitheater.[60] Those with social or family ties would fare somewhat better: Their remains would be collected by their loved ones and arrangements made in accordance with their beliefs and resources.

"So, what's the plan?" Camilla whispered to Heraklia as they made their way through the darkening streets of Londinium.

Lumbering in their wake were two barrel-chested youths from Pannonia, Rufus's latest acquisitions. The troupe master was always on the lookout for new fighting flesh—anything to get him out of the second-rate business of women gladiators—but Camilla could tell this pair was not going to be his ticket to fame and fortune. The boys were big, surely, but got confused if you turned a corner too quickly. This was going to be easy.

"We go to the temple, make our peace, and get back," Heraklia replied flatly.

"You can't be serious!"

"Where else are we going to go? Home to Daddy?" Heraklia shook her head, instantly regretting what she had said. "Rufus knows he has me. He wouldn't have let us out of his sight otherwise."

There was a weariness in her friend's voice Camilla had never heard before and it worried her. "This is all my fault. My father's just trying to get back at me. You don't have to go through with this. You're so close to buying yourself out already. It'll just take a little longer is all."

"Rufus is never going to let me retire."

It was a stunning revelation, too incredible to be true, but Heraklia continued, "I suspected as much when he kept putting me off, refusing to set my price, but today I was certain. He always fixes the draw and knew I was injured. He would never have set me up with Agave if he wasn't hoping she'd finish me off. Now that he's announced it in front of the entire company, he can't go back on his word. Whatever happens tonight, he'll have no more power over me." She caught Camilla's expression and laughed. "Don't look so surprised. The stars don't always revolve around you! Ah, here we are."

They stopped before a nondescript set of doors set into a high, blank wall, and knocked repeatedly until they heard the lock turn. The doors open slightly and a man with a shaven head peered out suspiciously.

"It's late," he said. "Come back in the morning when the goddess wakes."

But Heraklia was not going to be turned away. "We seek a special audience," she explained and made the secret sign, careful to hide it from the view of their escorts.

The priest looked between the two women and spotted Agave's pin in Camilla's hair. Recognizing them as true disciples whose need must undoubtedly be great, he opened the door wider to admit them.

When Rufus's goons stooped to follow, Camilla put out a hand to stop them. "Sorry, boys. Members only." And the door was shut in their faces.

Heraklia and Camilla stepped into the serene and fragrant domain of the Goddess Mother, she who answered to many names, but in this house would be known as Isis. The bald-headed priest led them across the open courtyard toward the shuttered temple that housed the statue of the goddess and her holy retinue.

The air was thick with familiar incense. Finding herself far from her home and her old gods, Camilla had long ago embraced this Queen of Heaven, who seemed to hold so much power in so many lands. She had found solace in the constancy of the faith's sights and sounds and smells wherever she traveled, but now the Egyptian goddess was here, too, and it was a thought Camilla found vaguely unsettling.

Nothing was as she left it, not the land, not the people, not the gods. Londinium could be any town in the empire. Everything she had loved, had fought for, was gone. This was her father's message. This was why he was sending Heraklia to her doom, to make his daughter see. Suddenly Camilla knew what she must do.

The two Pannonians looked up from their game of dice, surprised to see Camilla emerge so soon and without her companion. They were even more surprised when she pulled the delicate carved pin from her hair and jammed it forcibly into the door lock. But they did not actually think to run after her until she was down the block and rounding a corner.

⧕ 6 ⧕

"AT LONDON, IN THE TEMPLE OF ISIS"

In sharp contrast to the outrageous public displays of the amphitheater were the shadowy rites of the mystery cults. Born out of the cultural dynamism of the Hellenized East, these small minority sects were comparatively recent imports to the Italian peninsula. Although heavily influenced by the Greek, they retained much of the exotic flavor of their countries of origin—places like Egypt, Syria, and Iran—lands that must have seemed as distant and enigmatic to the average Roman as they do to most westerners today. Their core rituals and beliefs were closely guarded secrets, to be revealed only to the initiated. Not until fully inducted into the faith could a disciple hope to apprehend its central tenets, or "mysteries," teachings that held the promise of enlightenment, immortality, and earthly rewards in the hereafter.

With the discovery of three rare and seemingly unused lamps bearing the likeness of Anubis among the grave goods of Great

Dover Street Woman, one scholar has arrived at a different interpretation of the unusual assemblage. Historian Martin Henig believes the burial contains clues not to the occupant's profession, but to her religion. He asserts that the lamps, incense burners, and pinecones point to only one possible conclusion:

> When I first heard about the finds at Dover Street, I was absolutely convinced that we had the burial of a devotee of Isis.

As guardian and messenger of the gods, Anubis was a close companion of the goddess Isis, the preeminent female deity of the Egyptian pantheon. She, along with her consort, Serapis (a variant of the god Osiris), and their son, Harpocrates, comprised a holy trinity, representing the power of creation and the cycle of life, death, and rebirth. The trio had first been adopted and adapted from their original ancient Egyptian counterparts sometime during the country's Ptolemaic period, beginning in the late fourth century B.C., and arrived centuries later in Rome and the West as a mystery religion, gaining a wide following for its reassuring views of life after death.

The story of Isis and Osiris is an ancient one—a tale of betrayal, devotion, and renewal told for thousands of years before ever making its way to the Greco-Roman world. Its perhaps best-known rendition, however, comes not from an Egyptian, but a Greek: the philosopher and biographer Plutarch, a prolific writer on a multitude of subjects including history, ethics, and religion during the late first and early second centuries A.D. Having himself been a priest of Greek god Apollo at the cult center at Delphi, his treatise *On Isis and Osiris* delves into the practices and traditions of the

Egyptian-inspired sect in considerable detail, examining the precepts of the faith as allegories for more universal concepts of the divine.

Throughout the discourse, Plutarch refers to the Egyptian deities by their Greek names and sometimes equates them directly with gods from his native pantheon. To him, Amun was just another name for Zeus and Horus was what the Egyptians called Apollo. This was a reflection of both the process and product of religious syncretism, the assimilation of the beliefs of a culture, or cultures, by another. While the actual mechanisms for this phenomenon are hotly debated among modern scholars, it is apparent that conceptions of the gods could be very fluid and ideas flowed freely. Deities were routinely ascribed the appearance and attributes of others with whom they were seen to share traits, converging, conflating, combining, and recombining. In this way, Anubis was identified with the Greek Hermes to become Hermanubis, the figure portrayed on the three Great Dover Street lamps, with his jackal head and herald's wand (*caduceus*). As god of funeral rites, Anubis also had the task of escorting the dead before the king of the underworld for judgment. This was a role similar to that of Hermes in his aspect as *Psychopompus* ("Conductor of Souls"), a figure all too familiar to the gladiators as he appeared in the arena to verify the dead lying in the sand. Priests of Isis would take on the guise of Hermanubis in processions, donning a jackal mask and carrying Hermes' staff or palm frond, signifying the triumph of life over death.[1]

Some of these syncretic figures even gained sufficient recognition on their own to split off from the main and take on a life, and a following, all their own. This is seen most clearly in the ascension of Serapis, who was himself a Hellenized version of Osiris merged with another sacred figure of ancient Egypt, the Apis bull, to become an entity that outwardly resembled neither but possessed many of the powers the two held in common. In this new form, Serapis seems not to have supplanted Osiris from the narrative at the heart of the Isiac mysteries, but it is in his name, not his predecessor's, that most of the shrines come to be consecrated outside of Egypt.

Relating the key myths of the cult of Isis and Osiris, Plutarch first sets the stage by recounting the origins of the Egyptian pantheon.[2] He tells of how the sky goddess Rhea (known to the Egyptians as Nut) was said to have laid with the god of the earth, Cronus (Geb), and become pregnant by him. When her husband, the Sun (Ra), learned of the adulterous affair, he cursed the goddess that she should not deliver during any month of the year. But Rhea had an ally in the clever Hermes (in this instance, associated with the Egyptian Thoth), who was greatly enamored of her. He played a game of draughts with the goddess of the moon and won from her a small fraction—the seventieth part—of each period of her illumination. All told, his winnings amounted to an additional five days, which he added to the length of the calendar, bringing it from three hundred and sixty days to three hundred and sixty-five. This provided Rhea with the loophole she needed to give birth while staying true to the letter of her husband's commandment. On the first of the five days, Osiris was born, accompanied by much fanfare, as befitted a future king. His siblings followed in short order, including Isis (Aset), whom he later married, and Typhon (Seth), their constant foe.[3] Where Osiris's birth was auspicious, Typhon's was ominous, tearing himself prematurely from his mother's womb and springing forth from her side.

Divine yet mortal, Osiris reigned over Egypt as king, but did not limit his beneficence to his own people. He traveled the world, bestowing the knowledge of agriculture and civilization upon all humanity.[4] When not in residence, Isis ruled the kingdom in Osiris' stead, remaining ever vigilant against the machinations of the jealous Typhon. The couple's wicked brother was only biding his time, however. With the aid of seventy-two conspirators, Typhon hatched a scheme: He presented a magnificently crafted chest at a banquet where Osiris was in attendance and announced that he would give it to whosoever fit perfectly inside. Unbeknownst to Osiris, the box had been custom built to his exact measurements. Each partygoer clambered into the chest and tried it on for size, but came away disappointed. When it came to be Osiris's turn, he had no sooner lain down than all those involved in the plot rushed forward. They threw the lid closed and nailed the casket shut. The box was sealed with molten lead for good measure and then cast into the Nile, which carried it out to sea.

When Isis learned of Typhon's treachery, she went into a profound mourning and set out in search of her missing brother-husband-king. She roamed the earth, desperate for any sign. It was during her wanderings that she discovered the existence of the child Anubis, the son of Osiris by their sister, Nephthys. Herself the wife of Typhon, Nephthys had once come to Osiris in the guise of Isis and tricked him into making love to her. The result was Anubis, but Nephthys, fearing her own husband's anger, sought to expose the infant shortly after his birth. Isis found the abandoned child and he was raised to become the god's loyal attendant and protector.[5]

Isis' search ended when she received word that Osiris' wave-tossed casket had come to rest on the shores of Byblus. There, the box had been obscured from sight by thick vegetation until a tree grew around it, enclosing it within its mighty trunk. The great tree had attracted the notice of the local king, who ordered it to be cut down and installed as the roof pillar in his private residence. In order to gain access to the royal household, Isis ingratiated herself with the queen and was appointed nurse to the young prince. At night, the goddess would transform herself into a swallow and flit about Osiris' wooden prison, lamenting their fate. At the same time, she endeavored to confer immortality upon her charge by incrementally burning away the mortal elements of the child's body, but when the boy's mother happened upon this scene she became hysterical and the gift was never fully realized. It was then that Isis chose to reveal her true self and purpose. She demanded the pillar be taken down so that it might be split open and her husband's body recovered.[6]

Isis returned to Egypt with Osiris' casket and went to their son, Horus, to set him on the path to vengeance. On the way, she concealed the chest in a nearby woodland, but while hunting boar one night by moonlight, Typhon stumbled upon the box's hiding place.[7] Bent on thwarting a family reunion, he tore the corpse into fourteen pieces and scattered them across the earth. Once again, Isis set out in quest for her husband's remains, sailing around on a boat made of papyrus reed. In some versions of the story, she was joined by her sister, Nephthys, and Anubis, whose keen senses proved instrumental in the search.[8] Each time she came upon a piece of the body, Isis buried it with all proper ceremonies and honors, as though it was the whole. This is one of two theories given for the multiple "tombs" of Osiris located throughout Egypt. Each of these important cult sanctuaries claimed to be the true final resting place of the king, even though their numbers sometimes exceeded the number of available parts. The other possible explanation proffered by Plutarch is that all but one of the sites were ruses intended to keep Typhon from ever discovering the god's body again. The only piece Isis was unable to locate was Osiris' penis, which had been thrown into the Nile where it was eaten by fish. She fashioned and consecrated a replica to replace it. Once again complete, Osiris was able to advise his son from the underworld as Horus trained to avenge the wrongs perpetrated against his parents.[9]

Following his travails, the reconstituted Osiris became lord of the land of the dead, while Horus ruled the earthly kingdom in his stead. In Egyptian tomb art, Osiris frequently appears as a mummified king, tightly bandaged, wearing the tall white conical crown of Upper Egypt and grasping in crossed arms the crook and flail of office. Pharaohs became identified with this father-and-son pair. The reigning monarch was regarded the personification of Horus while his predecessor was Osiris, whom he too would become upon his own passing. Together, both gods and men represented the cyclical rejuvenation of the earth by the Nile. The river was the country's lifeblood, without whose annual inundation the land would be reduced to desert. Both destructive and restorative, this primordial force of nature was deeply incorporated into the Egyptian belief system and the waters of the Nile continued to play a central role in the rites of the cult as it spread far from the banks of the river that inspired it.

Another central theme to the originating mythos was the casting of Horus and Typhon as archetypal adversaries. In their conceptions as the Egyptian Heru and Seth, they embodied the eternal battle between light and dark, order and chaos, each necessary for the other to exist. This age-old conflict is often seen to mirror the struggle for supremacy between the early city-states of Upper and Lower Egypt. Once unified under a single ruler, however, the vicissitudes of politics seem to have taken their toll on the patron gods of the various centers. With their associations with pharaohs past and present, Osiris and Horus rose in esteem, while Seth's place in the newly aligned scheme became problematic and pushed to the periphery. Associated with warfare, upheaval, and the desert, Seth may have once been viewed as the opposite side of the same coin— a vital, albeit violent, force that paved the way for creation and renewal—but with the shift in attitudes, he became increasingly demonized, until finally he was equated with the monstrous Typhon of Greek mythology.

As the heroic vanquisher of Seth, Horus was an ancient figure whose origins and aspect appear to have become somewhat muddled over time. While Plutarch lists him as the second of the five offspring of Rhea, he also acknowledges that the falcon-headed god was the son of Isis and Osiris. He relates one explanation that attempts to reconcile these divergent traditions by having Isis and Osiris fall in love and couple while still in the womb, thus enabling the earth mother to give birth to both parents and child.[10] During his conflict with Horus, Typhon plays upon his enemy's confused heritage, accusing him of being illegitimate. It was an allegation the gods apparently took very seriously, but after weighing the evidence, they came to rule in Horus' favor. The situation is only complicated further when Plutarch goes on to describe how, sometime following his death, Osiris had visited Isis and conceived Harpocrates, who was himself the juvenile aspect of Horus, his name being a Greek interpretation of the Egyptian phrase meaning "Horus the Child."[11]

Outside of Egypt itself, Horus appeared most consistently as Harpocrates. It was in this incarnation that he was exported as a key component in the cult of his parents—the renewing cycle of life made manifest—and was frequently shown as a young child perched upon Isis' knee, poised to suckle. This image of mother goddess and child was not unique. The *Matres* of northwest Europe were often depicted with a babe or two at the breast. These infants do not appear to have been divine entities in their own right, however. They are merely symbolic accessories meant to signify fertility, a message just as easily conveyed with a lap full of fruits and vegetables or loaves of bread, the products of a bountiful harvest. More intriguing is the possible iconographic parallels between the figures of Isis and Harpocrates and the Madonna and infant Jesus. The similarities seem to extend beyond the superficial, sharing concepts in common such as the virgin birth and the holy child destined to become king and savior, sufficient evidence for some scholars to suggest the Egyptian cult exerted some influence on the burgeoning Christian faith.[12]

For her part, Isis remained a powerful and pivotal divinity throughout the history of ancient Egypt and was one of the few to endure even after the time of the pharaohs was long over. She was the giver of life, through whom all else was made possible. She restored Osiris and bore Horus. She was a kingmaker, the mother of gods and their divine representatives on earth, the pharaohs. Her original name, Aset, includes the hieroglyph for "throne," and depictions often show her wearing this sign upon her head like a high, stepped crown. Her most identifiable headdress, however, is the disk of the sun resting between a pair of long, sinuous cow's horns.

Little is known of her earliest worship. She appears repeatedly as Aset in the Pyramid Texts, some of the oldest extant Egyptian religious inscriptions. Most of these mortuary texts date to the fifth and sixth dynasties, a period that spanned several centuries during the mid–third millennium B.C., although earlier examples are known. These inscriptions appear as tightly packed vertical registers of hieroglyphs covering the inner chamber walls of pyramids belonging to both pharaohs and their queens alike at the Egyptian necropolis of Saqqara. Although hundreds of lines have been recorded and translated, their interpretation remains somewhat contentious, seeming to lack a clear linear narrative. They are thought instead to reflect the utterances of priests, sacred phrases recited during the funeral ceremony: hymns, spells, and prayers set in stone. All together, they are but mere glimpses into what was by that time already a sophisticated and full-blown belief system, speaking of the enduring spirit of the deceased and their ascent into the afterlife. Most of the elements of Aset/Isis' own story also appear to be in place by this time: her love of Osiris and bereavement over his loss, as well as her search, reassembly, and restoration of his remains.

Believed a great magician and wielder of considerable magics, Isis was a protector of both the living and the dead, curing the sick and watching over the departed along with Selket, Nephthys, and Neith. Small gilt statues of these four tutelary goddesses were found in the tomb of Tutankhamun, standing guard with delicate arms outstretched around the canopic shrine containing the internal organs of the mummified king. In other funerary contexts, she was often depicted with large, colorful wings extending from her arms. With these, she fanned the winds and imbued the breath of life back into the body of Osiris. The image of her kneeling with outspread wings was a protective symbol frequently seen in Egyptian tomb art.

Isis' sphere of influence also encompassed cultivated crops and all good things that came from them. She was the goddess of beer and bread and was believed to have invented the spinning and weaving of flax for linen clothing and canvas for sails.[13] Much revered by sailors, as *Isis Pharia* she was the patroness of the Pharos Lighthouse at Alexandria, one of the legendary Seven Wonders of the Ancient World.[14] Recent underwater expeditions off Pharos have led to the discovery of the submerged ruins of this once great landmark, which protected ships and guided them to the teeming port city.

The waters of the eastern Mediterranean had long facilitated contact and trade between the peoples along its shores, but the campaigns of Alexander the Great in the fourth century B.C. intensified the process: Greek ideas mingled with those of Egypt, the Near East, and even India, to produce a veritable kaleidoscope of religious belief. Following Alexander's death in 323 B.C., one of his Macedonian generals, Ptolemy I, took Egypt for himself. The dynasty he founded reigned supreme until 30 B.C., when Cleopatra VII, last of the Ptolemaic rulers, finally succumbed to Roman forces led by the future emperor Augustus.

During the Ptolemaic period in Egypt the role of Osiris was melded with that of the Apis bull, a sacred and oracular animal whose center of worship was the city of Memphis. Chosen for its special markings and believed to be an earthly incarnation of a god, the Apis was a powerful symbol.[15] Upon a bull's death, the sacred beast was mummified and buried with reverence in an enormous stone sarcophagus at nearby Saqqara, after which there was an extended period of mourning as priests scoured the land for a successor. Visiting dignitaries were expected to pay homage to the bull when in Egypt and terrible things befell those who did not show the proper respect. Herodotus relates how, in the sixth century B.C., the Persian king Cambyses was said to have killed a calf newly proclaimed the Apis and was supposedly driven mad for his crime.[16] Ancient Egyptian records, however, refute this tale, stating that no Apis died at this time and that Cambyses himself dedicated a sarcophagus for a mummified bull as befitted a conquering king who wished to be regarded as pharaoh. Alexander, too, made the appropriate sacrifices to the bull upon entering Egypt and his Ptolemaic successors made the cult their own.

Although not Egyptian in origin, the Ptolemies legitimized their rule by adopting many pharaonic traditions. Like Isis and Osiris and many earlier sovereigns of the land, it became customary for brothers and sisters to marry to maintain the potency of the royal line. As the right to rule was divinely conferred, they also came to observe the local beliefs, but with their own Hellenistic bent. Under the Ptolemies, Osiris and Apis became a single entity, "Osiris-Apis" or Serapis, with his cult center in the Ptolemaic capital of Alexandria. Thoroughly Greek in aspect, he was depicted as a powerful man with a mane of thick curly hair and flowing beard. Atop his head sat a *modius*, or grain measure, alluding to his authority over fertility and the agricultural growing cycle. In some representations, he was accompanied by the three-headed dog Cerberus, guardian of the gates of Hades, reinforcing his association with the Greek god of the underworld. A composite figure, he was also occasionally equated with other deities, both Greek and Roman, including Dionysus, Jupiter, and Aesculapius, but in terms of popular appeal, he was often overshadowed by his vivacious sister-consort.[17]

In his consideration of Egyptian beliefs, Herodotus equates Isis with the Greek Demeter, another mother goddess who was closely associated with fertility and cereal crops.[18] Parallels can be drawn from their two stories as well, both having scoured the earth in search of lost loved ones. In Demeter's case, however, it was her daughter Persephone, also known as Kore (meaning "maiden"), who went missing, abducted by the lord of the underworld, to rule as his queen. The bereaved Demeter neglected her duties and would not cause grain to grow until Persephone was returned, but because the girl had tasted the seed of a pomegranate while in death's realm, she could never be truly free of that place. A compromise was reached between the gods whereupon Persephone remained in the shadow lands with her husband for three months out of the year and spent the remaining time with Demeter. Only when mother and child were reunited were the fields allowed to sprout and ripen.

As in Egypt, the agricultural progression of sowing, germination, and harvest was seen as a metaphor for the human life cycle and inspired its own mystery religion. With its cult center in the Attic town of Eleusis in eastern Greece, the Eleusinian Mysteries celebrated Demeter and Persephone with elaborate festivals and rites open only to the initiated. Although men could join, the faith held a special appeal for women, with its female protagonists and a narrative evoking the social and physical transformation of a maiden into woman.[19] Unlike many other mystery cults that spread far and wide, the Eleusinian Mysteries remained very much rooted in its sense of place. To be fully inducted in the sect, devotees had to travel to Athens to participate in the initial days of the annual festival and then continue on in procession to Eleusis to undergo the initiation ceremony. Many, however, successfully undertook the journey and gained admittance, including the emperors Marcus Aurelius and his son Commodus.[20]

The notions of personal salvation and an idyllic afterlife for any and all were concepts ill defined, if not entirely lacking, in the Greco-Roman belief system. As a result, it had long been assumed that the mystery religions had initially been promulgated by outsiders—foreign slaves, freedmen, and traders—and quickly found a foothold among the more downtrodden and disenfranchised of Roman society. Many, including the cult of Isis, gained a reputation for attracting those along the margins: the fractious urban poor, the demimonde, the feckless, effete, and emotionally weak. Indeed, the more xenophobic members of the literary elite encouraged this perception, blaming much of the ills of society on the influx of people from the East with their decadent, superstitious, and decidedly un-Roman attitudes and practices. True to form, Juvenal was an outspoken proponent of this view:

> I cannot, citizens, stomach a Greek Rome. Yet what fraction of these dregs is truly Greek? For years now, eastern Orontes[21] has discharged into the Tiber its lingo and manners, its flutes, its outlandish harps with their transverse strings, its native tambourines, and the whores pimped out round the racecourse.[22]

More recent considerations of the subject, however, have refuted claims that the mysteries appealed foremost to foreign immigrants, shady and unsavory elements, and women of question-able morals. Studies of the epigraphic evidence show that adher-ents, in fact, ran the gamut of society.[23] Dedicatory inscriptions bear the names of men, women, even children, from all walks of life, including slaves and freedmen, but also merchants and ship owners, as well as highly placed military officials, civic administrators, and provincial governors. At times, the cult of Isis at Rome could count among its advocates members of the imperial family as well as sev-eral emperors.

The attraction of mystery religions was not only in their mes-sage, but also their methods, promising a more intimate, personal rapport with their gods. Unlike monotheistic faiths, these beliefs did not negate the validity of the official Roman religious system, but stood in compliment to it, offering more intense, revelatory encounters with the divine. Although priests or advanced members of the congregation might preside over ceremonies and interpret doctrine, all attendees were expected to take an active part in the proceedings. Being secret, most of the details of these rituals died with their last practitioner, but they are known to have included processions, banquets, music, dance, and song. Followers of the mysteries took on their obligations by choice and, through a shared body of knowledge, ritual, and experience, formed strong bonds within their exclusive, close-knit societies. These were notions that appealed to many who found the conventional forms of religious expression somehow wanting—too anonymous, rigid, distant—placing the welfare of the community above that of the salvation and perpetuation of the individual. Although conventional forms of worship could also include private acts of devotion, large public gatherings were the mainstay of traditional faiths of the time.

The Roman calendar was rife with *dies feriae*, holy days or holidays, set aside for the veneration of specific divinities of the expansive Roman pantheon. While sometimes incorporating *ludi*, public games and other entertainments were secondary to the main purpose of the *feriae*. This was a time for the people to renew their commitments to the gods and ensure their continued goodwill. The entire populace was expected to participate. The faithful brought offerings and attended services at the god's temple, while the less devout would, at the very least, refrain from working so as not to pollute the sacred day. The Roman calendar lacked the concept of a weekend, days of religious observance spaced at weekly intervals. Instead, these numerous, though irregular, *dies feriae* provided the people with a welcome respite from their labors.

Despite the solemn rites that often inaugurated these holy days, there was usually ample opportunity for merrymaking. The Saturnalia was one of the most anticipated events of the year. This festival was held in honor of the ancient god of seed and sowing, Saturn, around the winter solstice in the latter half of the month of December. The celebration could last up to a week, but always began on the seventeenth of that month with special ceremonies at the god's temple the Roman Forum. After the performance of animal sacrifices, a great public banquet was held. The days that followed were marked by the relaxation of many restrictions. All business ceased, and men shucked their cumbersome togas in preference for more colorful, informal attire and donned soft caps called *pillei*. Token gifts were exchanged and the ban on public gambling was lifted. Social roles could also be inverted for a time, such that masters served their slaves.

During the major rituals themselves, however, the role of the general populace tended to be that of passive observer, looking on as a cadre of priests and officials interceded with the gods on their behalf. It was a relationship reproduced in every Roman home, where it fell to the *paterfamilias* to conduct the rituals honoring the guardian spirits of the family. These protective gods of the household (*lares*) and pantry (*penates*) were furnished with offerings of food and prayer in order to secure their blessing for all who dwelled within. Often, a small shrine (*lararium*) containing their likenesses stood in the corner of the house's atrium, but the domestic hearth also served as a focus for their veneration. Rome, too, had its own sacred hearth, tended by the Vestal Virgins, a select group of women who spent the greater part of their life in service to the eternal flame of the goddess Vesta.

The Roman gods were not naturally inclined toward benevolence. Rather, their allegiance had to be won and maintained through ceremony and sacrifice. Failure to observe the prescribed rites or a flaw in their execution could result in the withdrawal of divine favor. Ceremonies had to be repeated if any sort of gaffe was detected, lest risk the wrath of the slighted deity. Those appointed or elected to the task of mediating between the gods and the people considered it a great honor and a grave duty, but for the majority it was not a full-time commitment. Few, other than the Vestals, whose purity requirements precluded them from fulfilling the traditional female roles of wife and mother, were expected to forgo a secular life. Instead, it was common for Roman priesthoods to be held by leading members of the community, who were still able to pursue public careers and private lives. Church and state were inextricably tied during this period and religious offices often served to open doors to even greater political influence. Following Julius Caesar's example, it became customary for emperors to be conferred the title of *pontifex maximus*. As chief priest of the state religion, the emperor held sway over the *collegium pontificum*, the governing body of priests and religious affairs.

Roman deities were little concerned with the spiritual well-being or moral rectitude of their suppliants. So long as all the correct rituals were observed, they would be appeased and could be expected to look favorably upon requests made of them. This reciprocal relationship was played out on all levels, from the state to the individual. Inscriptions on altars dedicated to the gods frequently bore the abbreviation VSLM, which stood for *votum solvit libens merito* or "gladly and willingly fulfilled the vow," indicating that the stone had been promised as payment for a prayer answered.

The exchanges between mortal and god took on a further legalistic air in the case of curse tablets, such as the hundreds of examples found at the sanctuaries of Sulis Minerva at Bath and Mercury at Uley in Britain. Thrown into wells or nailed to poles within the temple precinct, these small, tightly rolled lead sheets bear crudely scratched messages to the god of that locality asking them to take revenge on whosoever has wronged the petitioner, usually by stealing from them. If the person cannot put a name to the thief, they cover all possibilities, requesting that the perpetrator be accursed "whether slave or free, man or woman" with all manner of physical and mental ills until the missing item is returned. Frequently, the document transfers the ownership of the stolen object—usually an article of clothing or a bit of money, farm implements or livestock—to that god, thus ensuring the deity has a vested interest in recovering what is now their own property.

Such contractual relationships did not imply any long-term obligation on the part of either party, mortal or immortal. If one deity failed to heed a person's prayers, they were free to try another. For those whose survival was especially precarious, however, for whom there might be no chance of appeal, remaining in the continued good graces of the gods was an absolute must. For the gladiators, whose actions were steeped with symbolic meaning, the gods shadowed their every step. They accompanied the combatants in the *pompa* to the arena and heard the fighters' final pleas in shrines specially installed in the amphitheater. Mortals masqueraded as gods on the arena floor, signifying the sanction of the higher powers over the proceedings. Even still, many fighters sought to tip the balance with a little additional divine intervention. Their armor bore the images and attributes of their divine patrons, such as Jupiter, chief of the gods, Mars, god of war, and the heroic demigod Hercules. At the London amphitheater, a small molded figurine of a goddess was found near the threshold of the animal pen.[24] Excavators believe it had been placed there deliberately as a votive offering, possibly to Juno, wife of Jupiter, who in her aspect as Juno Curitis was the protector of spearmen.

Soldiers stationed along the fringes of the empire also availed themselves of a staggering array of deities. They paid homage to the divine spirit (*genius*) of the emperor and the official gods of the Roman state, but also brought the gods of their own provincial homelands with them to the remote frontiers. To these they added the names of the local divinities of the lands they currently occupied, just to hedge their bets, but perhaps most intriguing was the degree to which the military embraced the mystery religions.

For centuries, Hadrian's Wall in the north of England marked the limits of the civilized world. It seems an incongruous landscape for the worship of the Persian deity Mithras, but this god of truth and light was a particular favorite among the soldiery. His was the quintessential mystery cult. With a membership restricted to men only, these secret societies consisted of a hierarchy of seven grades, each requiring its own trials and rites of passage.[25] As an initiate progressed through the levels, the central mysteries of Mithras were incrementally revealed. The imagery of the cult was heavily imbued with astrological symbolism, including its central scene of the tauroctony, or bull slaying, which served as the focal point of worship. It shows Mithras, in his characteristic peaked Phrygian cap, sacrificing the divine bull from whose blood all living things were created.

The basic plan of a Mithras temple, known as a *mithraeum*, appears to have been much the same throughout the Roman world. Known examples tend to be long, low, and arched, sometimes partially, if completely, subterranean. Three *mithraea* have been identified along the length of Hadrian's Wall, at Carrawburgh, Housesteads, and Rudchester. The relatively close proximity of the forts at Carrawburgh and Housesteads and the modest size of the nearby *mithraea* suggest that congregations were drawn from a very localized area and could not have been very large, as rites were conducted inside these cave-like structures, rather than just outside in a sacred precinct like most other religions of the time. The main altars and tauroctony scene were always located at one end of the *mithraeum*'s long axis, opposite the entrance. Flanking a central aisle running the length of the temple were raised platforms upon which followers would recline for services and ritual meals.

Like Mithras on the British frontier, Isis and Serapis also seem to have found homes among the soldiers posted at border sites along the Rhine and Danube.[26] Both cults drew worshippers from all ranks, high and low, just as they did civilians from every rung of the social ladder. There would seem, however, to be a common thread among the professions they attracted. Soldiers, sailors, merchants, and government administrators, while not lowly or marginal members of society, were still, in a sense, outsiders within the local community. Transplanted and transient, these individuals may have sought acceptance and fellowship among others of their ilk within the cohesive and personally oriented mystery faiths.

The rites and revelries of these cults were considered strictly private affairs, but the authorities occasionally felt compelled to step in when what went on did not remain behind closed doors, especially if the cult members' actions were seen to threaten community welfare and social stability. Livy recounts the scandal that rocked Rome and led to the suppression of the notorious Bacchanalia by the senatorial decree in 186 B.C. The Bacchants, the legendary female celebrants of the Bacchus, god of wine, had already been immortalized for their ecstatic and frenzied woodland rites by the playwright Euripides in the late fifth century B.C., but the reputation of the god's followers had not improved with time:

> A great part of them are women, and they are the source of this mischief; then there are men very like the women, debauched and debauchers, fanatical, with senses dulled by wakefulness, wine, noise, and shouts at night.[27]

Rumors of the corruption of youths led to an investigation and interrogation of the cult's members. Livy provides a litany of crimes the group was suspected of perpetrating under the cover of piety:

There was not one form of vice alone, the promiscuous matings of free men and women, but perjured witnesses, forged seals and wills and evidence, all issued from this same workshop: likewise poisonings and murders of kindred, so that at times not even the bodies were found for burial.[28]

While the Bacchanalia was an extreme example, historical accounts show the Roman Senate, and later the emperors, repeatedly attempting to rein in the rapid rise of a number of mystery religions, including that of Isis. Officially leery but at the same time privately fascinated by all things foreign and exotic, Roman attitudes toward what Suetonius refers to as "that fickle superstition" appear to have been rather changeable, particularly during the cult's early years.[29] Temples to foreign gods were not allowed inside Rome's *pomerium*, the sacred confines of the city. This did not seem to deter Isis' more ardent followers who, according to the historian Dio Cassius, built more than one shrine in her honor—some at great personal expense—within this exclusive precinct. Such indiscretions did not escape the notice of the Senate, who ordered the demolition of all temples of Serapis and Isis within the bounds of Rome in 53 B.C.[30] Dio goes on to say that it was some time before devotees felt comfortable professing their faith in public, but Valerius Maximus records an incident in 50 B.C. that contradicts this claim.[31] At that time, the tenacious sect seemed to have once again incurred the Senate's wrath with more unauthorized construction, but public sentiment already seemed to be changing. Workmen at first balked at destroying the temple until a consul himself took up an ax and battered at the doors himself. While yet another illegal sanctuary had to be dismantled in 48 B.C., the pendulum had swung and five years later

Rome's leaders relented, sanctioning a temple to be built beyond the *pomerium* on the Campus Martius.

Originally an open plain consecrated to the god Mars, the Campus Martius ("the field of Mars") came to house any number of important structures, including the Pantheon, dedicated to all gods, and Augustus' Ara Pacis, the Altar of Peace, as well as the emperor's own mausoleum. The plan of the sprawling *iseum-serapeum* complex at Rome is recorded in the Severan Marble Plan, an enormous stone map of the city dating to the reign of Emperor Septimius Severus (A.D. 193–211). Shielded from public view by a high perimeter wall, the precinct was made up of a number of structures, including the main temple of Isis containing the cult statues and a colonnaded sanctuary dedicated to Serapis, as well as accommodations for priests and priestesses, attendants and pilgrims. The magnificence of the compound is attested by two enormous marble sculptures representing personifications of the Nile (now in the Vatican Museum) and the Tiber (in the Louvre). A giant gilt bronze pinecone, possibly modeled after that of the *Pinus pinea*, or stone pine, was also found just outside the complex. Once part of a fountain dating to the first or second century A.D., it now stands as the centerpiece of the Cortile della Pigna (Courtyard of the Pinecone) at the Vatican and lent its name to the square where it was found (Piazza della Pigna).

A scaled-down, but extremely well preserved version of an Isis temple, or *iseum*, was uncovered at Pompeii in 1765. Nestled against the outer curve of the Large Theater, the complex presented a blank face to the street, surrounded by a high wall with an offset door that did not allow the casual passerby a view into the inner sanctum. Once inside, the wide colonnaded portico surrounding the courtyard constrained the space around the temple, making it appear somewhat outsized. In one corner of the courtyard also sat the *purgatorium*, a small unroofed structure with a short flight of interior stairs that led to an underground shrine housing sacred waters of the Nile in a stone basin. Like its counterpart in Rome, the compound also contained several side rooms to accommodate the faithful in residence. The main hall was decorated with paintings of ethereal Egyptian landscapes and scenes from myth. On its huge stone table were found the preserved remains of a last meal, laid out but uneaten, a testament to the town's last dark day. The priests had waited until too late to abandon their beloved temple. Their bodies were found out on the streets where they fell as they tried in vain to spirit the sacred emblems and temple treasury out of harm's way.[32]

As was often the case with fringe sects that gained official recognition to become more accepted and established, many of the cults' rituals and beliefs became public knowledge, although their initiation rites and deepest mysteries remained well-kept secrets. In his *Metamorphoses*, the second-century-A.D. philosopher and rhetorician Apuleius provides a description of the morning ritual at the temple of Isis. Attendants, both male and female, would prepare the statue of the goddess by dressing her in sacred garments, carefully securing the "Isis Knot" in the folds of cloth between her breasts. This symbol, which resembles the ankh, the Egyptian glyph for "life," was also worn by priestesses of the goddess, while priests shaved their heads and wore long linen kilts, tied about the chest. Once the goddess was ready to greet the day, she was "awoken" by hymns sung in Egyptian and the music of flutes and *sistra*, metal rattles with horizontal slates that slid from side to side to produce a sound when shook. The doors of the temple were opened, revealing the goddess to the assembled congregation who honored her in song and prayer while the priests performed sacrifices and poured libations of holy Nile water.[33]

In addition to the daily rites, the cult celebrated two major annual festivals. March the fifth marked the *Navigium Isidis*, or "Vessel of Isis," the start of the sailing season. Festivities began with an entertaining procession of groups in costume: men dressed as women, soldiers, gladiators, hunters, fishermen, philosophers, and so on. Animals in outlandish getups were also led in parade, followed by women scattering flower petals and perfume. Then came the main body of worshippers carrying lamps, torches, and candles, along with musicians and singers, as well as those to be newly initiated into the group. The novitiates were dressed in new linen robes, the women veiled and the men with cleanly shaven heads. Priests carrying the sacred emblems of the sect then preceded the gods themselves—attendants carrying their images as well as priests in their guise, wearing masks such as that of the jackal-headed Anubis. When they reached the docks, a new boat with a white sail was loaded up with offerings, sanctified, and set adrift. Then the entire procession wended its way back to the temple where worshippers ascended the steps of the *iseum* and kissed the feet of the goddess. Prayers were offered and the sailing season was officially opened.[34]

A much more solemn occasion was the autumn festival, called the *Inventio*, which reenacted episodes from the Isis and Osiris myth as a passion play. Over the course of several days, from the twenty-eighth of October to the third of November, priests and followers alike joined their goddess in her bereavement over her lost husband. They dressed as mourners and sang laments, beating their chests with pinecones in their grief until they drew blood. The search for Osiris' dismembered remains was performed with a priest taking on the part of Anubis to root out pieces of a disarticulated statue scattered throughout the sanctuary. On the last day, the parts of the Osiris statue would be reassembled and the congregation would rejoice at the return of life to the god and the land.[35]

That these beliefs eventually reached the far-flung shores of Britain seems incontrovertible. An altar dedicated by the third-century Roman governor of Upper Britain, Marcus Martiannius Pulcher, commemorates the restoration of a temple to Isis. The inscription suggests the aged structure had fallen into disrepair and was in a much-ruined state by the time the governor came to its rescue.[36] The location of this temple, or *iseum*, has yet to be determined, however. Martiannius Pulcher's altar was found reused as a building block in a later Roman riverside wall at Blackfriars in London, having been dismantled and removed from its original context. Other religious artworks met the same ignominious end, including a relief depicting four *Matres* figures.[37] The recycling of these stones may correspond with Constantine's promotion of Christianity in the early fourth century A.D., which prompted a great many rival beliefs to dissolve or go to ground.

Numerous small finds related to the cult also attest to the presence of followers of Isis in Britain, and Londinium in particular. Among the objects that have come to light is a carved gemstone (*intaglio*) incised with the image of the goddess and her symbols, as well as small cast statuettes of the goddess and Harpocrates, the youthful incarnation of the Egyptian Horus. Isis' son is instantly recognizable for the long curl of hair that falls about his right ear, often called a "Horus Lock." This was a style worn by many royal offspring during the Egyptian dynastic period and was later revived for child initiates of the cult. Sometimes bordering on the cherubic, Harpocrates was frequently portrayed holding the chubby little index finger of his right hand to his mouth, an attitude leading some to believe him the god of silence and secrecy. Although such an attribution might seem fitting for a central figure in a mystery religion, the gesture, like the Horus Lock, was a holdover from a much earlier time, when they were traits commonly used to denote children in ancient Egyptian art.

Another personal item likely to have belonged to a devotee of Isis was a recently "rediscovered" bone hairpin. Originally found in 1912 at Moorgate Street and now residing in the collections of the Museum of London, the long, fragile object is missing a portion off its end, but its ornately sculpted head remains intact. Exquisitely rendered, with great attention to detail, the shaft of the pin transforms into an arm, adorned with a tiny snake-headed spiral bracelet, and culminates in a hand holding aloft the bust of a goddess on the tips of its individually carved fingers. With her high headdress and elaborate hairstyle, this figure was initially thought to represent Cybele, the "Great Mother," whose cult had originated in Asia Minor but who, like Isis, had passed through Greek hands and gained a widespread following during the Roman Empire as a mystery religion. Upon reconsideration of the headpiece, later scholars have found it to more closely resemble a device worn by Isis than any associated with Cybele.[38] Whereas Cybele typically sported a low, mural crown, reminiscent of crenellated city walls, this was determined to be a somewhat simplified version of one of the most prevalent emblems of the goddess Isis: the solar disc set between a pair of cow's horns. Dating to the first or second centuries A.D., this lovely yet functional item of personal adornment would have been a subtle declaration of the wearer's faith as well as a way of keeping the protective goddess always close.

Another piece of evidence suggests that the sect's arrival in London may have been quite early in the town's history, almost two centuries prior to the dedication of the Martiannius Pulcher altar and nearly contemporary with the later first century date of Great Dover Street Woman. A ceramic flagon bearing the inscription *Londini ad Fanum Isidis* ("At London, in the Temple of Isis") was recovered from Tooley Street in Southwark. Roughly dated to around A.D. 75, the vessel's largely intact state suggests to Martin Henig that it did not have far to travel before being carefully committed to the earth, either as part of a burial or some other form of ceremonial deposition.[39]

The fact that both the inscribed flagon and the Anubis lamps of the Great Dover Street burial were found in Southwark may be more than mere coincidence, according to Henig, perhaps indicating that the as yet undiscovered London *iseum* was located somewhere in that vicinity. For the Museum of London team, however, faith alone is not enough to account for all the burial's unusual aspects. It does not, for example, explain why this woman, while elaborately mourned in death, seems to have also been subject to social exclusion. Isis worshippers were not necessarily outcasts from society. In the eyes of Jenny Hall, both interpretations could be true:

It is possible that we have here a wealthy and influential follower of the goddess Isis but who is also a female gladiator. The one possibility doesn't rule out the other. It could be a combination of the two.

With its popular, widespread following and promise of deliverance in the afterlife, the cult of Isis may well have appealed to a gladiatrix—a woman who dealt in death.

The sun had dipped below the horizon by time Camilla reached her desti-
nation. She had lost her pursuers with ease many streets back, but they
would have given up the chase before it started had they known where she
was headed.

The excited buzz coming off the amphitheater told her it was still full to
capacity. The hour was late and the last of the headlining acts had long since
been cleaned off the arena floor, but no one dared leave their seats for fear
of missing the surprise finale.

In the whirlwind of last-minute preparations backstage, no one seemed
to notice Camilla. She made her way through the fray toward the tunnel
mouth where a pair of nervous-looking horses stood, harnessed to a rickety
two-wheeled rig. A long spear and oval shield were already loaded onto the
back of the cart. Perfect.

"Camilla? Where's—" It was Myrine, dressed in something that approx-
imated a Roman soldier's uniform, cobbled together out of bits from the

company's spare armor box. She was carrying a blanket heavily patched with mismatched fabrics and a helmet to which someone had attached a mass of dark red yarn, no doubt stolen off a dyer's drying line.

Camilla was in no mood for explanations. She grabbed the items out of Myrine's hands and mounted the cart, fastening the blanket about her shoulders like a cloak. The younger woman grabbed her arm.

"Camilla, you can't. This is madness!"

"Are you going to stop me?"

The look in Camilla's eyes told Myrine there would be no stopping her. She stepped back and watched as Camilla sent the horses tearing down the tunnel.

There was the drumming of hoofbeats and the rattle of wheels, and suddenly a terrible cry split the darkness of the arena. Many in the audience recognized the sound immediately, although it had not been heard for a very long time: the ancient call to arms of the Britons. A nervous hush fell over the spectators as they strained to locate its source.

Attendants, thinking they had missed their cue, rushed across the sands. Torches flared to life and the crowd gasped as a hurtling chariot appeared and disappeared between the pools of light. And, there, driving the horses, could it be? A warrior woman with hair like blood, clothed in a cloak of many colors. It was a chilling effect, but no more so than when the apparition careened to a halt in the center of the ring and addressed them in the old tongue.

"My people," came the booming voice. It echoed so tremendously off the high walls of the amphitheater that Camilla almost did not recognize it as her own. "Too long have you slept under red roofs. You have forgotten the old ways, forgotten who you are. You have let the Romans have their way with your lands and your children." She caught sight of her father shifting uneasily in his seat. A little more realistic than he bargained for, perhaps? "But it is not too late to restore what has been lost, to reclaim that which you abandoned so long ago."

Anxious murmurs spread through the stands. Camilla's speech had struck close to home for more than just one of their number. It was at that moment that the rest of the troupe, all done up as soldiers, entered the arena. The audience's reaction to their appearance was at first difficult to gauge, but as Camilla defeated her sisters-in-arms, one after the other, the mood gradually began to shift. By the time she faced Myrine, the last to step forward, the crowd's discomfort had turned to anger.

Camilla managed to catch the girl under the chin with the edge of her shield and sent her tumbling, unconscious, to the ground. Standing alone amidst the carnage, Camilla turned toward the tribunal and removed her helmet. Whatever spell had gripped the audience when she first rode out was now well and truly broken. How dare this mere woman—this gladia-trix—try to shame them? The same people who had demanded her life be spared just hours ago were now on their feet, baying for her blood.

Her father, too, was standing, but his expression was one of, what, sor-row? Regret? Had he really believed this ridiculous farce was going to show her the error of her ways and send her rushing into his arms, begging his for-giveness?

A cheer went up amongst the crowd and Camilla could see another fig-ure stalking across the field toward her. Heraklia. The woman was livid. Jaw set, sword clenched in one white-knuckled fist, she launched herself at Camilla without a word.

Camilla put up as much of a fight as she could but had nothing left in reserve. She was soon driven to the ground under Heraklia's furious onslaught.

"It didn't have to be this way!" Heraklia spat as she stood over her.

"No, this is exactly how it had to be," she replied. Hair plastered to her face and struggling for breath, Camilla raised a hand to the tribunal.

Her father flinched at the gesture for mercy as though it were an accusation of guilt. Gradually, he looked past it to meet her desperate gaze. It was as though he were seeing her for the first time, his battered and bloodied child. For the briefest of moments, it seemed as though he would do it, would redeem himself before all these people. But then he heard the shouts all around him and dropped his eyes. He lifted his arm unsteadily and slowly turned his thumb. The stands erupted.

There were tears in Heraklia's eyes when Camilla knelt before her. Her friend could not know why she had done it, but she would understand soon enough.

Heraklia kissed her on the top of the head. "See you in the next life," she whispered.

"I'll be waiting," Camilla replied, and the roar of the crowd fell away.

7

THE DEATH OF A GLADIATRIX

Not every gladiator who entered the arena was assured a violent demise, even in defeat. According to Michael Fulford:

> Gladiatorial contests didn't necessarily end in death. It depended on the crowd, it depended on the circumstances, it depended on the individuals and how they had fought and so both gladiators could have left the games unharmed and lived to fight another day.

Inscriptions record numerous instances of such temporary reprieves. Occasionally, if a pair was so evenly matched and performed with such exceptional bravery and skill that neither could gain the upper hand, a draw might be called and both would be dismissed from the field (*stans missus*) having been awarded the palm frond of victory. Only in battles fought *sine missione*, without quarter, was it an absolute requirement that one of the competitors exit through the Gate of Libitina. The show's organizers set such ground rules in advance, so that both gladiators and audience alike knew mercy was not an option. Fighters would have to press on despite exhaustion, incurring grievous injuries, until one emerged the decisive victor. Considered overly cruel and excessive by Augustus, the emperor attempted to ban these especially vicious contests, but the prohibition did not last.[1]

The actual survival rate of gladiators is difficult to determine. Sufficient data on which to base statistical assessments are lacking, but experts believe they can discern some general trends. A study conducted by Georges Ville examined the recorded results of one hundred gladiatorial duels from the first century A.D. He suggests that, at the outset of a match, a fighter had a heartening 90 percent chance of coming away alive. Of course, it was the winners of these pairings who constituted the bulk of that number. For those who did not fight to a stalemate but lost outright, the outcome was somewhat less promising. About one in five was doomed to perish, either there on the spot or later of their wounds, even after their request for a stay had been granted. This proportion of fatalities is considered to be somewhat on the low side when compared to prior or subsequent centuries, however. It may be that, as with Augustus' interdiction against contests *sine missione*, clemency was more the norm during this period and the ultimate penalty was reserved for those whose performance was subpar or otherwise failed to please. In later centuries, the overall potential for survival dropped precipitously to 75 percent, with half those defeated having been killed. Marcus Junkelmann sees this as indicating a fundamental shift in attitudes, where the death of the loser came to be expected and *missio* was only meted out as a reward for surpassing valor.[2]

Even in victory there were no guarantees, however. Although physicians like Galen prided themselves on reducing gladiator mortality through their ministrations, it was not unheard of for fighters to succumb to their injuries, regardless of having won or lost.[3] One such unlucky individual had the dubious honor of claiming the title *invictus*, unconquered in death.[4] Notices for gladiatorial shows held at Pompeii further attest to the existence of substitutes, fighters waiting in the wings to take the place of a combatant if they became too badly hurt to continue. Called a *tertiarius* or *suppositicius*, fighters such as these were most likely to be deployed in the event of a sudden disabling injury that threatened to cut the entertainment short. This might be an attraction worth advertising to assure attendees of a good show, but it did not bode well for the participants.

Professional gladiators who had just fought a long, hard battle would not normally be required to face a fresh opponent immediately. There was little honor in taking on someone already bloodied and spent. It was hardly "sporting." Only the *noxii*, condemned criminals whose execution was the intent, were regularly forced to square off against successive adversaries until their sentence was carried out. Dio Cassius does recount one episode in the life of Caracalla when the emperor ordered a gladiator named Bato to fight three men in a row, resulting, predictably, in his death.[5] That Dio thought this a remarkable incident, illustrative of Caracalla's murderous nature, suggests that this was a rare occurrence. Caracalla even appears to have felt some obligation to the dead man afterward, as he was said to have given Bato a magnificent funeral.

Few fighters seem to have been as honored in death as they were in life, however. Although they could rise to great heights through their performance, Roman society appears to have had little use for a dead gladiator. Gurneys, the "couches of Libitina," sat ready and waiting along the sidelines to whisk the bodies of the fallen from the arena. These would be removed to the *spoliarium*, a kind of charnel house, for processing. Likely derived from the term *spolia*, referring to the spoils taken during war, corpses were brought to this place to be stripped of their weapons and armor.[6] Any items of value would be returned to the *ludus* or *familia* that had supplied the equipment. As property themselves, gladiators' lives were no more their own than the swords in their hands.

The mutilated corpses, polluted by blood and violence, faced one further indignity at the *spoliarium*. Seneca insinuates that it was routine for their throats to be slit once out of the public view.[7] Although most would have received the coup de grâce from their opponent while still in the arena, this final defilement was necessary to confirm that those so fated were not still clinging to life and to ensure none attempted to fake their death as a means of escape.

While the location of these facilities has yet to be identified archaeologically, some believe that chambers for this purpose were incorporated into the structure of the Flavian Amphitheater itself, either just beyond the Gate of Libitina or amongst the labyrinthine underground cells and tunnels beneath the floor of the arena.[8] A late Roman document does identify the presence of a *spoliarium* a short distance from the amphitheater, somewhere in the vicinity of the Caelian Hill. Individual schools may have also maintained their own separate facilities. An inscription associated with the Ludus Matutinus, the school in Rome devoted to the production of fighters for the wild animal hunts, makes reference to several members of staff, including a manager (*curator*) of the *spoliarium*. That such a job existed suggests that it was a sizable operation, requiring the supervision of a body of personnel dedicated to its grisly business.[9] With historical records indicating that the dead could number in the tens, hundreds, and sometimes thousands in the case of lavish imperial spectacles in the capital city, it is not inconceivable that many of these way stations for the slain existed throughout the city.

Considering the multitudes known to have met their end in the arena, there is comparatively little extant evidence regarding their final deposition. A mere scattering of gladiator tombstones survives throughout the empire, hardly representative of the masses who were slaughtered. In the whole of Italy, less than sixty funerary inscriptions associated with this profession are known.[10] Of these, the majority comes from Rome, unsurprising since the capital would have had the greatest demand for these fighters' services. However, most of the remainder were found associated with ancient towns to the north, not what one would immediately expect given the reputation of the gladiator schools to the south, particularly around Capua and the rest of the Campanian region.

Any number of theories can be proposed to explain the seeming discrepancies in the quantity and distribution of these monuments. It can be assumed that memorials of all kinds, not just those of gladiators, once existed in much greater numbers than have been recovered to date. Time takes its toll on even the most durable of substances, either through natural weathering processes or direct human intervention. Throughout the centuries, it has been common practice to redress and reuse quarried blocks from derelict structures whose significance has long since been lost. Inscribed stones from the Roman period have been found built into riverside embankments, the foundations of garden sheds, and even the walls of later churches. It is a rare thing to be able to match a Roman gravestone with its grave, as so many of the markers were moved from their original context in antiquity or by later antiquarians.

Nor was stone the only option for denoting a burial site. Very often less permanent materials were used, such as wood or ceramic, which would have been preserved only under the most fortuitous of circumstances. The commissioning of a carved stone could be a protracted and costly endeavor, and in the lowly and uncertain life of the gladiator, neither time nor money might exist in any great abundance. Instead of asking why there are so few memorials to gladiators, the real question might be why are there any at all. The paucity of evidence for the lasting commemoration of the fallen may indicate that the practice was the exception rather than the rule, and that the majority of those cut down in the amphitheater would have more routinely joined the ranks of the anonymous and disregarded dead.

Even without the arena as a source, ancient urban centers waged a constant battle against accumulating corpses. Extreme poverty and high mortality rates meant many died alone or abandoned. Congested Roman cities employed public undertakers to organize the transport of bodies beyond the city limits. These government contractors collected fees for their services and were heavily regulated, as handling the dead was fraught with anxieties about both physical and spiritual contamination. Work gangs engaged to carry off the bodies of the condemned were, for example, required to drag them along the ground by hooks while wearing red and ringing bells.[11] Even with the provision of mortuary specialists, the numerous edicts passed dictating the proper disposal of the dead and assessing steep fines for scofflaws suggest illicit dumping was a continual concern. Both the writers Varro and Horace refer to public cemeteries in the area of the Esquiline Hill, which at the time fell outside the bounds of the ancient city. There, bodies could be tossed into large communal pits (*puticuli*), cursorily buried or burned with little or no ceremony.[12] Many of the *noxii*, by contrast, received no burial at all but were left to rot on public display or hastily discarded into the Tiber where the river would carry their taint far from decent folk.[13]

There can be no doubt that the social stigma of *infamia* also followed the gladiators to their graves. An inscription from Sarsina (ancient Sassina), in the Umbria region of Italy, suggests that some citizens were especially particular about with whom they bedded down for all eternity. The text states that one Horatius Balbus donated to the town the private land around his tomb for use as a public cemetery, with the stipulation that no "unworthy" individuals be allowed burial there. These undesirables included shameful suicides who had died not by the sword but by the noose, and those involved in immoral trades such as prostitutes and gladiators, whether freeborn or freed.[14] Persons of high rank who signed on as *auctorati*, contract gladiators, may have been especially singled out for exclusion. A senatorial decree dating to A.D. 19 from Larinum implies that these disgraced members of the elite could have been penalized for their poor choice of profession by denial of burial, just like a common criminal.[15] Such a dire prohibition may have been intended to make those of high birth think twice before committing themselves to such an ignominious fate.

For most Romans, to be refused a decent burial was quite literally a fate worse than death. In retribution for his brutality and innumerable abuses during his life and reign, the emperor Commodus was posthumously sentenced by the Senate to the most terrible punishments that could be exacted upon the dead: the obliteration of his name and memory from the public record (*damnatio memoriae*), the denial of burial, and the ruination of his corpse. Because of his penchant for the arena and spectacle, it was demanded that his body be treated like that of a gladiator: dragged through the dust on a hook, violated in the *spoliarium*, and finally thrown into the Tiber like so much human refuse. It caused a terrific uproar when it was discovered that the late unlamented ruler had been secretly interred during the night.[16] So important was it to observe the funerary ritual that someone was willing to risk the wrath of the entire Senate for as execrable a character as Commodus.

In Roman and Greek traditions alike, it was believed that the spirits of the deceased would not rest easy unless all the proper rites were performed. Individuals who could made provisions for their own demises well in advance, drafting wills and even commissioning their own memorials, but it would ultimately fall to their heirs and intimates to see their final wishes carried out. For slaves and other dependents, it was the duty of the head of the household to see that they were provided for in accordance to their station. Some cherished servants and freedpersons even rated their own niche in the family crypt.

Those who lacked the connections of *familia* or sufficient resources of their own might instead turn to organizations expressly created to fill this need, called *collegia funeraticia*.[17] These burial societies represented informal financial compacts between its members and were not officially sanctioned by the government, which generally regarded private clubs with suspicion but tended to look the other way in this instance. These groups appealed mostly to those of the lower orders, especially slaves and freedmen, and were often composed of individuals involved in the same craft or trade. The members met regularly and their gatherings may have had a certain social or religious component as well, but the dues that were collected were earmarked primarily for funeral expenses. With their combined assets, they were able to act in concert, finalizing arrangements when one of their number had passed and constructing communal sepulchers. These tombs often took the form of a *columbarium* (literally, a "dovecote"), a partially or wholly subterranean chamber whose walls are punctuated with row upon row of niches into which urns containing cremated remains were placed.[18]

Roman society's ambivalent and dissociative attitudes toward gladiators carried over into the fighters' treatment in death. Celebrated yet reviled, noble yet servile, gladiators lived in a world apart, segregated from the general population by the walls of the *ludus*. Within these tightly constrained and controlled environments, bonds were forged despite the risks involved, if not because of them. It must have been a strange and grim kind of solidarity, in some ways reminiscent of the esprit de corps of the military and in others the bleak desperation of the penitentiary. It was this unlikely band of associates, however, that came forward to claim the bodies of their own once they had served their purpose and the public had tossed them aside.

Although some gladiators were known to belong to their own *collegia*, such as the one from the Via Labicana dedicated to Silvanus, god of the groves,[19] the mortuary role of these clubs has not been explicitly proven. More often, it was the deceased fighter's friends and comrades who stepped in to play the part of community and kin, if not the owner of the *familia gladiatoria* or the sponsor of the games in which the fighters had perished. The altruistic intentions of the latter are somewhat suspect, however, as their own names were often emphasized above those of the deceased, suggesting the monuments were more self-serving acts of aggrandizement on the part of the dedicator than generous tributes to those who had died in his name.[20]

More heartfelt, it seems, are the simple sentiments articulated by those who cast themselves as the peers and relations of the departed. Although a gladiator's status should have precluded him from having a family, it seems that some were able to manage it nonetheless. Quite a few inscriptions speak of wives and children who set up monuments to their "well-deserving" and "dear" gladiator husbands and fathers. One woman, named Laurica, now widowed with two young daughters, proudly boasts of her *secutor* husband's fame and prowess, noting that he had been *primus pilus* and that the fans celebrated his spirit, although his opponents may not have been quite so fond as, she warns, whoever he defeated, he killed.

It is difficult to estimate what proportion these domestic relationships represented among the larger gladiator population, since commemoration was traditionally the obligation of the surviving heirs, and thus the sample may be skewed toward those who were in a position to form familial bonds. In all likelihood, however, such unions were not officially recognized while a gladiator was still under contract. This is reminiscent, in many ways, of Roman soldiers who were prohibited from marrying until the completion of their term of service, but nevertheless seem to have had consorts and progeny installed in the civilian settlements that inevitably sprung up outside forts. Some gladiators may have delayed starting a household until retirement following a glorious career, but this does not account for all. Many inscriptions handily provide both the fighter's age at death as well as the number of years spent with the devoted wife who had arranged for the gravestone. Several appear to have begun their relationships when the fighter was in his mid- to late teens—perhaps predating his commitment to the arena, but perhaps not.

How and why some gladiators merited commemoration while so many others went unacknowledged is a matter of much speculation. In her surveys of gladiators' epitaphs from Italy and the city of Nîmes in southern France, Valerie Hope interprets these memorials as representing a community apart—a social microcosm that served to approximate the network of relationships denied its members in the outside world.[21] Such allegiances were possible even within the largest of gladiator schools. A funerary inscription from Rome attests to the loyalty that one, a *murmillo* from the Ludus Magnus, felt for a late comrade who was a *retiarius* at the school and whom he called his *convictor*, or "messmate." Frequently, these brothers-in-arms register their emotions at the loss of one of their number by characterizing the death as undeserving or premature. There are expressions of betrayal and deceptions by fate.[22] In one instance, a fighter who had come up against the same opponent on two prior occasions and who was said to have spared his life both times was himself killed by this ungrateful foe the third time they faced one another.

Those individuals able to integrate themselves into this society of outcasts seem to have been more likely to be remembered after they were gone. Although many epitaphs list the age to which a fighter lived, the number of battles fought and won, and whether his freedom (*liber*) had been granted as matters of pride, a long and illustrious career does not seem to have been a prerequisite for the acknowledgement of his peers. One unfortunate, named Macedo, was memorialized by his fellow Thracians after having died as a *tiro* in his very first match at the age of twenty.[23]

In her study of the collection of fourteen gladiator gravestones from Nîmes, Hope observes that several of the monuments were found grouped together within a larger cemetery, not far from the town's amphitheater. All of the stones dedicated to fighters recovered from the site were also of a fairly consistent type: simple, unadorned, round-topped *stelae* displaying the most basic of inscriptions. Coupled with additional evidence for the uniformity of monuments in Spain and southern Gaul, as well as the physical clustering of memorials at Split in the former Yugoslavia, a picture begins to develop in which commemoration of the dead was employed as a means for expressing group affiliation and collective identity. Socially restricted while they lived, gladiators barred from some burial locations may have shown preferences for others, forming communities in death as they did in life.[24]

Not all gladiators' gravestones were humble affairs, however. The range of elaboration could vary widely and may in some ways have reflected the differential status of the fighters they represented, but one must be careful when making such determinations. Very often, customs of commemoration can and did change over time and geography. While individualized and ornate memorials may have been all the rage at one place and time, solidarity through simplicity and conformity could have been the rule in another. Decoration of a gladiator's monument might take the form of anything from schematic depictions of the tools of their trade—arms, armor, and accolades, such as the *corona*—to representations of the deceased in full regalia. These "portraits," however, differed significantly from the skillfully executed busts so often commissioned to adorn the tombs of wealthy Romans. Shown full body with all their equipment, occasionally even wearing helmets that covered their faces, it seems the primary intent of these images was to convey an impression of the deceased's occupation rather than to provide a realistic and recognizable portrayal of the individual.

Stripped down to its bare essentials, it was the inscription that was the most important component of these monuments. Epitaphs summarized the key defining features of a person's life and career as their heirs and associates wished them to be remembered. Gladiators were typically identified by their name and fighting style, but often precedence was given to the latter, possibly in a bid for legitimacy through the celebrity conferred by their profession. In addition to their age and honors, fighters' epitaphs also tended to include their origins since they were a particularly mobile population, drawn from far and wide, who met their ends far from their places of birth. One fighter named Thelyphus was careful to note that, although he appeared in the arena as a Samnite, he was in fact a Thracian by birth.

As with most Roman tombstones, gladiators' epitaphs often began with the initials D M, or were addressed the full phrase *Dis Manibus* ("to the Spirits of the Dead"). While the gods ruled from on high, the dead were seen to inhabit a world belowground. There were few universally held beliefs among Romans about what followed death beyond a general acceptance—a hope, at least—that the soul persisted beyond the existence of the body. The notion of an immortal essence, the *anima*, or "breath of life," was one shared with the Greeks. To philosophers who contemplated its elusive nature, such as Plato and Aristotle, it represented the divine spark that distinguished the animate from the inanimate. In addition to this intrinsic and ineffable life force, humans were thought to possess more discrete and definable spirits. Unlike the *anima*, however, these entities were not thought to be solely restricted to living beings.

The *numen*, the embodiment of the will or consent of the gods, could inhabit a person as well as a place and even personify an abstract idea, such as virtue or loyalty.[25] It was a concept not altogether different from that of the *genius*, which at first served to symbolize a man's procreative power but was later also conferred upon groups and localities. Troops stationed at Hadrian's Wall dedicated altars to the *genius* of their units, as well as that of the local area, the garrison, and the commander's house. In a Roman household, family members paid tribute to the *genius* of the *paterfamilias* as progenitor and protector, including slaves who swore oaths upon this guardian spirit.[26] Emperors uncomfortable with the notion of being venerated as living gods, as was the custom in much of the eastern portion of the empire, resolved this dilemma by encouraging the worship of their *numen* and *genius* in their stead. Only upon an emperor's passing and apotheosis, his ascent into the heavens, would he be deified, thus prompting the deathbed declaration attributed to Vespasian, "Alas! I believe I am becoming a god."[27]

For most mere mortals, however, there was decidedly less to which to look forward. There was little to recommend in the classical views of the afterlife: At best, the deceased's immortal essence might gain admittance to the shadowy realm of the underworld and, at worst, it might be shut out or condemned to a period of torment for some terrible offense to the gods. Upon their passing, a person's spirit was also thought to join the ranks of the *manes*, the shades of the dead. These noncorporeal and rather listless beings were believed to linger by their place of burial, where they awaited the visits of their surviving relations and the offerings of food and wine they would bring. Such spirits could turn vengeful if not regularly and properly attended, returning to haunt the living as ghosts, or *lemures*. This was a particular concern when a person died without kin to perform the appropriate duties to the dead.

In a society for whom family and lineage was paramount, Romans were careful to honor and respect their departed ancestors and loved ones. This began with the funeral itself, a ceremony that often took several days to complete, but there were also a number of different days devoted to both the public and private veneration of the dead. The foremost festival was the *Parentalia*, an eight-day period in February during which parents and other close kin were remembered. Other sacred days also included a memorial component, such as the *Rosalia*, a feast that took place in the spring when the roses were in bloom and their petals could be scattered across the graves. The anniversary of a person's death was also a time for commemoration. Even the *lemures* had a festival, the *Lemuria*, in May, but this was less a day in their honor than a time in which certain rites were performed to protect the household from their mischief.[28]

Friends and kin would remain close at hand when a loved one lay on their deathbed. As the person expired, the nearest relation would bestow upon them a last kiss, hoping to catch the departing soul in their final breath. The deceased's eyes would then be closed and the family would take up a lament, repeatedly calling the dead by name. The body would then be cleaned and dressed, and a coin placed in the mouth to pay the ferryman Charon for their passage across the River Styx into the underworld. Without Charon's fee, it was believed the soul would be stranded on the opposite bank, unable to cross over. For the more well-to-do, the body might lie in state in the receiving room (atrium) of the house for some time, so that the person's many dependents and clients might pay their respects. The funeral itself began with a procession (*pompa*), in which the body was carried on a bier from the house, accompanied by family and friends all dressed in black. The procession often took place at night by torchlight, wending its way out of the city to the family tombs that lined the roads or, if the body was to be cremated, to a place where a pyre awaited. Throughout most of the Roman period, both cremation and inhumation were practiced, but prior to the third century A.D., cremation was the preferred method while inhumation predominated in later centuries.[29]

Based on the wealth of material recovered from the grave, Great Dover Street Woman's own funeral ceremony must have differed significantly from those of her neighbors, most of whom were interred in a more simple, if not downright haphazard, fashion. Her careful and elaborate cremation with its intriguing assemblage of grave goods clearly sets it apart from those surrounding in the humble burial ground. This has led Hella Eckhardt to arrive at a conclusion similar to that of Martin Henig regarding the burial and its occupant:

I think it might indicate someone who has beliefs that are different from the majority of the population maybe, eastern beliefs, quite possibly. Because the same combination of objects—lamps, incense burners, and burnt pinecones—also occurs in a number of temples of eastern deities.

Although seemingly unusual and exotic, the mortuary rite and associated artifacts are not, in and of themselves, wholly unique. All have been found to have parallels elsewhere in Britain. Even the Anubis lamps, considered exceptionally rare for the region, have two counterparts known from other sites. Instead, it is the quantity of objects in combination with the burial rite that distinguishes this discovery.

Cremations *in situ*, or "in place," while fairly infrequent in Britannia, were a more commonly observed phenomenon on the continent. As of a 1991 survey of Romano-British mortuary practices, the number of *bustum* burials, where the pyre had been built directly atop the burial pit, numbered only a couple of dozen or so and were found scattered throughout the province. Robert Philpott, who conducted the study, looks to a much closer inspiration for this rite than the distant East, however. He points to the local traditions of Germany, Gaul, and possibly Pannonia (modern Hungary) and posits that the custom may have been introduced along with military regiments whose complement had been raised in those areas.[30]

The inclusion of lamps and *tazze* is also not unknown from other British burials, although no other single grave seems to have produced quite so many examples. The inordinate number of these two vessel types found with Great Dover Street Woman suggests to Eckhardt a ritual of "intense light and purifying smells." Philpott would seem to concur, noting that lamps appear to have been restricted primarily to cremation burials and, as such, likely had more to do with the funerary ceremony itself than any intention of use by the deceased in the afterlife. He notes that most of the lamps recovered from these contexts seem to have been obtained new with the intent of lighting only once at graveside and then depositing within the pit. This may also be the case for the Great Dover Street examples, although no soot residue was found to indicate they had ever been lit. The tiny flame these vessels produced could have held any number of meanings for those in attendance, including replicating in miniature the function of the pyre itself: to purify and release the human spirit through cleansing fire.[31]

The burning of incense in *tazze* as a means of purification is also a recurring theme among cremation burials and it is not uncommon for lamps and *tazze* to be found in close association in these contexts.[32] A late-first- or early-second-century-A.D. marble relief from the Tomb of the Haterii family on the Via Labicana outside of Rome attests to the connection of these vessels with the funeral ceremony. A richly dressed lady is shown lying in state, well attended by musicians and mourners while two *tazze* sit alight on the floor at either end of her funeral couch.[33]

Despite the sheer quantity of material recovered from the grave at Great Dover Street, there is very little that connects objects with occupant beyond the symbolic act of the funeral ceremony. While personal possessions were often buried alongside a body, none of the items here assembled appear to have been used by the deceased during her lifetime. The lamps are new and *tazze* were hardly common household items, and certainly not in a set of eight.

There is a well-worn adage among archaeologists that the dead do not bury themselves. The manner in which the deceased is treated not only reflects how they were perceived in life, but is also thought to say much about those left behind. Choices of how to prepare the body, what to include in the grave, and the ceremonies and rites performed are decisions most frequently left to those nearest and dearest, whether related by blood or shared experience. By these choices, mourners attempt to articulate the role that the individual played within their social network, but through this group act of commemoration, also negotiate and reproduce their own collective identity. The need to recognize and reinforce such bonds appears to have been just as important, if not more so, among the marginalized communities of the gladiators as it was the wider society from which they were excluded.

Slowly, a line of torches made its way through the deepening twilight, across the bridge and away from the city. It was a solemn procession, accompanied by a measured drum, doleful flutes, and the gentle jangle of bronze rattles.

The company was led by three priests, their heads shaved, wearing long linen kilts. They sang hymns in a language no one else there understood, punctuated unnervingly by the loud wails of women bringing up the rear.

The professional mourners were probably a bit much, thought Heraklia, as she walked silently behind Camilla's draped and garlanded bier somewhere in the middle of the crowd. So determined had she been to give her friend a send-off in high style that money had seemed no object.

Funny that, she thought. Wonder if I'll ever get used to having money? No doubt, but by then there probably won't be any left.

She gazed into the glowing embers of the pinecones smoldering in her ceramic cup. Behind her trailed the seven remaining members of Rufus' rapidly dwindling troupe, each carrying a similar vessel. She was glad he had permitted them to attend the funeral, although Heraklia had given him a powerful incentive in agreeing not to press for the winnings she knew Camilla had left her in her will. It was enough that she was finally in possession of what was rightfully hers.

That woman had thought of everything, hadn't she? By setting the sentiments of the audience squarely against her, Camilla had paved the way for Heraklia to step in and play the hero. Everyone was so grateful to her for silencing their guilty conscience that they demanded Heraklia's release on the spot. Rufus could not refuse, and Camilla's own father had to foot the bill to free the woman who had killed his daughter. Truly inspired. The only flaw being that now she had no one with which to share her good fortune.

The procession turned off the road and began to navigate the uneven ground of the humble cemetery. She regretted not being able to obtain a piece of prime frontage for the burial, but no one would dare allow the likes of a gladiatrix to rub elbows with the spirits of their dear great-uncle Lucius or auntie Aelia.

When she caught sight of the great pyre, however, she was much cheered. The priests had done well in making the arrangements. It would be a beautiful ceremony.

For her part, Heraklia had made sure each of the familia had been provided with a small lamp to place in the grave after the fires had burnt themselves out. For those among them who had been initiated into the faith, the lamps bore the symbol of Camilla's guardian into the next world. The others were plain, but Myrine had asked if she could bring her own. When Heraklia spied it among the other assembled offerings, she wondered at its meaning. Who was the fallen gladiator pictured on the lid? Was it Camilla or did it symbolize something more?

Myrine was standing by the pyre, her eyes red-rimmed from more than just the smoke of the incense. The child had witnessed much in a short time, seen them at their worst and at their best, but the path she chose from here would have to be her own.

Some movement by the shrine at the far corner of the cemetery caught Heraklia's eye. A cloaked figure lurking in the shadows. Was this a father's remorse at last? Would he now take the torch from her hand and fulfill his final duty to a daughter?

But the figure did not step forward. With a sigh, Heraklia turned and thrust the brand into the pyre. In the morning, they would both be reborn: Camilla, in the embrace of the goddess, and she, on the road that would take her the farthest away from here.

Conclusion

Since the announcement by the Museum of London Archaeological Service, experts have been weighing in with their opinions on the identity of Great Dover Street Woman. Was she a gladiator? A worshipper of Isis? The pieces of the puzzle have been assembled and reassembled to produce any number of interpretations—views that some would consider mutually exclusive but which others have little difficulty in reconciling. Speculation will no doubt continue to rage around this enigmatic discovery, as definitive answers are rarely forthcoming in archaeology. Hypotheses can only be drawn on the basis of existing evidence and, in the case of Great Dover Street Woman, that evidence speaks less directly to the life she lived than it does to how she was regarded by the people and the society she left behind.

Kathleen Coleman cautions against an overreliance on any one component of the burial when making a determination, and expresses particular concern when it comes to the significance of the gladiator picture lamp. Vessels such as these were ordinary household items, mass-produced in workshops throughout the ancient world in an astounding array of styles and decorations. Scenes from the most popular entertainment of the day, she adds, were hardly an uncommon theme. In a town with an amphitheater designed to accommodate one-third of its total population, the sight of a gladiator might have seemed almost pedestrian. At best, Coleman is willing to concede the presence of the fallen gladiator motif suggests that the deceased, or else someone in her close circle, was an aficionado of the games and felt it an appropriate image to include in the funeral ceremony.[1]

Others are obviously willing to go much further in their interpretations, but not based solely on the evidence of one vessel, or even three. The inclusion of so many Anubis lamps, an otherwise rare type for the province, may have served as the inspiration for the alternative religious explanation offered by Martin Henig, but he also points to the use of *tazze* and pinecones to corroborate his theory of an exotic and imported ritual. In his survey of British burials, Robert Philpott notes a correlation between lamps and incense burners with cremation practices and mentions finds of pinecones in a smattering of other graves but does not relate these to any specific cultic customs.[2] While he does make a case for a foreign introduction of the *bustum* cremation rite, the connection he sees is a largely military one that leads him only across the Channel for its source.

The attribution of the burial to a member of the Isiac faith does not, in itself, account for the most perplexing aspect of this discovery: its apparent exclusion from others of its quality and wealth.

Here was a woman who had been buried with obvious deference and care in an elaborate and costly ceremony, but who had nevertheless been denied the company of the esteemed dead. The gleaming tombs of London's rich and famous lined the approaches to the rising provincial center, yet she was consigned to the background. In a world that so valued connections and kin, why was this individual kept at a distance?

There is little to indicate that followers of Isis were denigrated or ostracized simply on the grounds of their beliefs. Although the promise of deliverance in the afterlife might have appealed to the lowly and oppressed, this mystery religion had been attracting adherents from every social stratum for some time before the death of Great Dover Street Woman. The cult had gained particular clout during the reign of Vespasian and his sons, collectively known as the Flavian emperors, in the late first century A.D. Before Vespasian even took Rome, the priests of the temple harbored his teenage son, Domitian, during a tumultuous night in A.D. 69, enabling the young man to escape the city and the murderous supporters of his father's rival in the guise of a member of the congregation. The Flavians may have felt a further obligation to the faith after Vespasian was so well supported by the East in his bid for the purple, and later minted coins depicting the temple of Isis on the Campus Martius.[3]

Respected, yet not respectable: This was the inherent contradiction that would have to lie at the heart of any solution to the Great Dover Street riddle. There were certainly avenues to wealth and notoriety available to women that lay outside the bounds of propriety, but in the estimation of the archaeologists of the Museum of London, only one profession carried with it any illusion of honor and legitimacy—that of a gladiatrix. Such a controversial conclusion would send shock waves through the academic community and captivate the public. It would appear that the idea of a woman who fought is just as compelling now as it was nearly twenty centuries ago.

Romans felt a terrific ambivalence when it came to gladiators. They were inferior yet noble, powerless yet strong, slaves who were admired by emperors. A physically commanding woman, the gladiatrix must have held a disquieting allure for Roman men, in the view of Catherine Edwards:

> A female gladiator is a hugely paradoxical notion for Romans. The spectacle of an athletic, confident woman wielding a sword might well have been found exciting in all sorts of different ways for the Roman male viewer. Such a figure is perhaps embodying the worst fears of the anxious Roman male: Is this what's really lurking inside every apparently demure Roman female, the gladiator waiting to get out?

That women could and did perform in the amphitheater is borne out convincingly in ancient art, literature, and law. That some of these came from rank and privilege and actively chose to risk their lives would seem almost inconceivable, but this too has been demonstrated. The traditional ideal of the Roman matron was a world apart from a woman who put her body on display in the arena, embraced masculine virtues, acquired masculine skills, and took pleasure in providing base entertainment. Perhaps this dramatic role reversal provided these determined few with a semblance of the power and freedoms that their gender was otherwise deprived by the expectations of society.

What these women love is the sword.[4]

For all its double entendre, Juvenal's snide remark can be taken to refer to more than just those whose passions were enflamed by gladiators; it also serves to describe those women for whom the vicarious thrill was not enough.

Highborn or low, a gladiator's origins mattered little in the end. Whether by compulsion or choice, in committing to that life—however short—a person would be forever changed. Separated from kin and country, they took on new names and new physicalities. Their professions became their identity and their comrades-in-arms their family. The lucky few might have the opportunity to remake themselves once again from hard-won rewards drenched in blood, but whatever class she emerged from, a gladiatrix would have ended her days as an outcast among outcasts. Not unlike the young and wealthy woman buried in Roman London, with artifacts that link her tantalizingly back to the amphitheater.

NOTES

Abbreviations

   CIL = *Corpus Inscriptionum Latinarum*
   SIG = *Sylloge Inscriptionum Graecarum*

CHAPTER 1: Discovery

1. Drummond-Murray and Thompson 1998
2. Tabard Street was itself formerly known as Kent Street.
3. This funerary practice was more frequently observed on the Continent (Mackinder 2000: 13).
4. Signs of the pyre structure might have also been evident at the other end of the pit but a complete investigation was not possible due to the outlying location of the grave and time constraints (Mackinder 2000: 12).
5. Giorgi 2000: 65
6. However, Giorgi (2000: 65) argues that these trees may not have sufficiently matured in time to produce cones for the late-first-century-A.D. date of the burial. More likely, he concludes, the examples used in this instance would have been imported.
7. Turcan 1996: 80

8. Wardle 2000: 28

9. For more on the various categories of gladiator, see chapter 4.

10. Swan 1988: 18

11. Hall 1996: 82

12. Mackinder 2000: 37

CHAPTER 2: Goddesses, Amazons, and Warrior Queens

1. Statius, *Silvae* 1.6.51–56

2. Suetonius, *Lives: Domitian* 4.2

3. Tacitus, *Annals* 15.32.3, trans. Grant 1989: 360

4. Martial, *On the Spectacles* 7, trans. Ker 1968: 17

5. Juvenal, *Satires* 6.104–105, trans. Lefkowitz and Fant 1992: 32

6. Tacitus, *A Dialogue on Oratory* 29

7. Juvenal, *Satires* 6.266–267

8. Martial, *Epigrams* 5.24.10

9. *CIL* 7.1335

10. A festival honoring Flora, goddess of flowers and spring, believed a particular favorite among prostitutes.

11. Juvenal, *Satires* 6.246–264, trans. Ramsay 1940: 103–105

12. Evans 1991: 131

13. Dio, *Roman History* 76.16

14. Vesley 1998: 91

15. Dio, *Roman History* 66.25

16. Martial, *On the Spectacles* 8, trans. Ker 1968: 19

17. Petronius, *Satyricon* 45.7

18. Caesar, *The Conquest of Gaul* 4.33, trans. Sanford 1982: 102–103

19. Bulfinch 1947: 228

20. Virgil, *Aeneid* 1, trans. Knight 1986: 42

21. Davis-Kimball 1997: 45

22. Strabo, *Geography* 11.5.3, trans. Jones 1961: 237

23. Apollonius Rhodius, *Argonautica* 2.987–992, trans. Seaton 1930: 169

24. The other two deities the comprised the Capitoline Triad were Jupiter, leader of the gods, and Juno, his wife and queen.

25. Virgil, *Aeneid* 7, trans. Knight 1986: 200
26. Bulfinch 1947: 278–279
27. There is a slight discrepancy among ancient authorities as to the exact date.
28. Tacitus, *Agricola* 15, trans. Mattingly 1970: 65
29. "Boadicea," a variant of Boudica's name popular among nineteenth-century poets, is an incorrect Victorian invention.
30. Dio, *Roman History* 62.2, trans. Cary 1968: 85
31. Ibid., 83–85
32. Tacitus, *Agricola* 16, trans. Mattingly 1970: 66
33. *CIL* 6.920
34. Tacitus, *Annals* 14.32, trans. Grant 1989: 328
35. Ibid., 14.33, 329
36. Dio, *Roman History* 62.7, trans. Cary 1968: 95
37. Tacitus, *Annals* 14.35, trans. Grant 1989: 330
38. Dio, *Roman History* 62.2, trans. Cary 1968: 83

CHAPTER 3: Roman Women: *Virgo, Matrona, Lupa*

1. Livy, *Early History of Rome* 3.44–3.48
2. Except in the case of children born of female slaves, who were themselves slaves. If freed by the head-of-household (who may or may not have been their actual father), they would take the man's family name in accordance with the custom of the manumitted.
3. Soranus, *Gynaecology* 1.60
4. A physician rarely attended a childbirth, as most were men and often prohibited from directly examining a woman.
5. Hanson 1999: 34
6. The frequency with which this occurred is difficult to determine. Engels (1980) argues that high rate of female infanticide would have had a significant detrimental effect on overall population.
7. *Oxyrhynchus Papyrus* 744
8. *CIL* 4.294
9. Also known as the dies *nominum* or *nominalia*.

10. This was merely the convention, of course. Over time, it became fashionable to append additional *nomina* and *cognomina* to reflect an individual's illustrious heritage, including family names of the maternal line (Hanson 1999).

11. Rome's wars with Greece and its colonies early on in the empire's history led to a preference for slaves from these areas. Romans held the Greek language and culture in high regard and slaves from Greece and its former territories tended to be literate and skilled.

12. *CIL* 6.19128, trans. Gardner and Wiedemann 1991: 105

13. Publilius Syrus, *Maxims* 659, trans. Gardner and Wiedemann 1991: 47

14. Pliny the Younger, *Letters* 6.3

15. Golden 1988

16. *CIL* 14.1731

17. Pliny the Younger, *Letters* 5.16, trans. Lefkowitz and Fant 1992: 194

18. Ibid.

19. Pliny seems to have misspoken when giving the girl's age. Municia's epitaph is known and it indicates she was nearly thirteen, not fourteen, at the time of her death (*CIL* 6.16631).

20. Girls of poor families would not have been sent to school and usually lacked basic literacy skills. They would have been put to work at an early age on the homestead or in the family business. Epitaphs of two nine-year-old girls from Rome show one was employed as a spinner of gold thread (*CIL* 6.9213) and the other as a hairdresser (*CIL* 6.9731).

21. Pliny the Younger, *Letters* 4.19.2–4

22. Juvenal, *Satires* 6.434–456

23. Juvenal, *Satires* 6.287–289

24. Sallust, *Catilinarian Conspiracy* 25, trans. Shelton 1998: 297

25. *CIL* 6.10230, trans. Fantham et al. 1994: 318

26. The most conspicuous exception being the Vestal Virgins, who were exempt by custom, law, and the dictates of their office from many aspects of women's roles.

27. Balsdon 1998: 182–183

28. Possibly a symbolic reenactment of "bride-stealing" and/or an allusion to the Roman foundation legend of The Rape of the Sabine Women.

29. Sesterces: silver coins. Juvenal, *Satires* 6.136–137, trans. Ramsay 1940: 93

30. Gladiators, too, were included among the ranks of the *infamis*.

31. These intervals were later amended by the *lex Papia et Poppaea* (the Papio-Poppaean Law) of A.D. 9 to two years after a husband's death and eighteen months following a divorce.

32. The "three-child right" (*ius trium liberorum*) applied to freeborn women. The later *lex Papia et Poppaea* extended similar privileges to freedwomen who had produced four children.

33. Whether this was by choice to avoid further risks from childbearing or due to the fact that men preferred to marry much younger women is not clear (Frier 1999: 93).

34. Tacitus, *Annals* 15.23, trans. Grant 1989: 355

35. Nappo 1998: 65

36. For more on this event, see chapter 5.

37. Etienne 1992: 78; Grant 1971: 74

38. Will 1979: 37

39. Ibid., 38

40. *CIL* 10.810, trans. Fantham et al. 1994: 333–334

41. *CIL* 10.813, Ibid., 334

42. *CIL* 10.816, trans. Lefkowitz and Fant 1992: 300

43. *CIL* 4.1136, trans. Shelton 1998: 65

44. This differs from the ancient Greek tradition, in which women led a cloistered existence in special women's quarters in the home, cut off from the world outside.

45. The Fullery of Stephanus on the Via dell'Abbondanza is the largest such operation in town—even the atrium of what was previously a town house is given over to apparatus. In another fuller's workshop installed in a private home (Pompeii, VI.14.21–22), production activity appears to be more centered towards the peristyle at the back of the structure.

46. *CIL* 4.7862, 4.7863

47. *CIL* 4.8203, 4.8204

48. Although early excavators were eager to see signs of Roman decadence

around every corner and identified as many as thirty-five brothel sites in Pompeii, more recent estimates conservatively place the number of purpose-built establishments at nine, with seven of those being simple, single-celled offerings (Laurence 1994: 73).

49. Flemming 1999: 45
50. Pliny the Younger, *Letters* 6.16, 6.20
51. Today, volcanologists use the term Plinian to refer to these eruptive columns.
52. The couple was found with several pieces of jewelry, among these two gold bracelets, each weighing about one pound, in the shape of coiled snakes with jeweled eyes. One bears the inscription *"Dominus suae ancillae,"* leaving little doubt as to the relationship of this unfortunate pair. From http://news.telegraph.co.uk "Pompeii dig reveals gift to exslave girl" (9/12/00).

CHAPTER 4: The Life of a Gladiator
1. Pompeii, IX.1.12
2. Petronius, *Satyricon* 45
3. Auguet 1994: 151
4. *Scriptores Historiae Augustae* 18.7–11
5. Wiedemann 1995: 103
6. Evans 1991: 131
7. Juvenal, *Satires* 8.200–206, trans. Green 1998: 67–68
8. Petronius, *Satyricon* 117, trans. Grant 1967: 31
9. Grant 1967: 31
10. Kyle 1998: 84
11. See chapter 7.
12. *CIL* 6.631
13. Grant 1967: 39
14. Cicero, *Letters to Atticus* 4a, trans. Winstedt 1956: 283
15. Martial, *Epigrams* 11.66
16. Vegetius, *Epitome of Military Science* 1.11, trans. Milner 1996: 12–13
17. See chapter 2.

18. Suetonius, *Lives: Julius* 26.3
19. Martial, *Epigrams* 5.24, trans. Ker 1968: 377–379
20. Petronius, *Satyricon* 45, trans. Grant 1967: 31
21. Livy, *Rome and Italy* 9.40.17, trans. Radice 1987: 276
22. For a discussion of the origins of Roman gladiatorial combat, see chapter 5.
23. Junkelmann 2000: 37
24. Polybius, *Histories* 18.41, trans. Andrae 1991: 63
25. Junkelmann 2000: 47
26. Suetonius, *Lives: Claudius* 34
27. Petronius, *Satyricon* 45, trans. Heseltine 1969: 91
28. Cicero, *Tusculan Disputations* 2.17.41, trans. King 1966: 191–193
29. Juvenal, *Satires* 6.110
30. *CIL* 4.4353
31. *CIL* 4.4342
32. *CIL* 4.4356
33. *CIL* 4.4345
34. Martial, *Epigrams* 5.24, trans. Ker 1968: 377–379
35. *CIL* 4.1184
36. Grant 1967: 7
37. Suetonius, *Lives: Claudius* 34

CHAPTER 5: Blood Sport
1. Juvenal, *Satires* 10.81
2. Grant 1967: 7–8
3. Somewhat confusingly, the Latin word for a gladiator school and public games are one and the same: *ludus* (although games are consistently referred to in the plural, *ludi*). This catchall term can mean, among other things, a play, diversion, or show, or a place of exercise or practice.
4. Homer, *Iliad* 23.170–177
5. Virgil, *Aeneid* 11, trans. Knight 1986: 281
6. Herodotus, *Histories* 4.71–72

7. As quoted two centuries later by Athenaeus; Wiedemann 1995: 30

8. Weidemann 1995: 31

9. Futrell 1997: 12

10. Junkelmann 2000: 38

11. Grant 1967: 12

12. Futrell 1997: 19

13. Ibid., 204–205

14. Grant 1967: 11

15. Wiedemann 1995: 6

16. Köhne 2000: 17

17. Wiedemann 1995: 7

18. Plutarch, *Crassus* 8

19. Grant 1967: 26

20. Lefkowitz and Fant 1992: 215

21. Futrell 1997: 110–118

22. Junkelmann 2000: 38–43

23. Ibid., 34

24. Pliny the Elder, *Natural History* 36.116–120

25. Brothers 1995: 115

26. Bateman 2000: 36

27. The *lex Julia theatralis* as described by Suetonius (*Lives: Augustus* 44)

28. Futrell 1997: 164–166

29. Suetonius, *Lives: Caligula* 26

30. Ewigleben 2000: 136

31. *SIG* 802

32. Plato, *Laws* 833d

33. Ewigleben 2000: 136

34. Prudentius, *Reply to Symmachus* 2.1094–1098, trans. Thomson 1953: 93

35. Suetonius, *Lives: Augustus* 44

36. Auguet 1994: 35

37. Köhne 2000: 20

38. Ibid., 19

39. Wiedemann 1995: 110–111

40. Grant 1967: 49

41. Auguet 1994: 176

42. Dio, *Roman History* 73.18–19

43. Wiedemann 1995: 3

44. Bateman 2000: 35

45. Josephus, *The Jewish War* 7.37

46. Tacitus, *Annals* 15.44, trans. Grant 1989: 365

47. Ibid., 366

48. Tarpeia was said to have asked for what the Sabines bore on their arms in payment for her collusion, thinking she would receive bracelets of gold, but was instead crushed under the weight of their shields.

49. Seneca, *Letters* 70.19–21, 23

50. Ibid., 7.2–5, trans. Shelton 1998: 355

51. Auguet 1994: 101

52. Suetonius, *Lives: Nero* 12

53. Quintilian, *Major Declamations* 9.6, trans. Shelton 1998: 357

54. Auguet 1994: 55

55. Tacitus, *Annals* 14.17, trans. Grant 1989: 321–322

56. Junkelmann 2000: 68

57. Auguet 1994: 55

58. Bateman 2000: 33

59. Junkelmann 2000: 69

60. Auguet 1994: 166

CHAPTER 6: "At London, in the Temple of Isis"

1. Witt 1971: 199

2. Plutarch, *Isis and Osiris* 12 (355E–356)

3. Somewhat confusingly, Plutarch lists Horus as the second offspring born to Rhea; however, Horus is also considered the son of Isis and Osiris. The goddess Nephthys (Nebhet) was the fifth and final child born in the days won from the moon.

4. Plutach, *Isis and Osiris* 13 (356B)

5. Ibid., 14 (356F)
6. Ibid., 15–16 (357–357C)
7. Ibid., 8 (354)
8. Witt 1971: 198
9. Plutach, *Isis and Osiris* 18 (358–358B)
10. Ibid., 12 (355F)
11. Ibid., 19 (358E)
12. Witt 1971: 216–217
13. Ibid., 16
14. Turcan 1996: 79
15. Herodotus, *Histories* 3.27.1
16. Ibid., 3.30.1–3.38.1
17. Hornblower and Spawforth 1996: 1355–1356; Ferguson 1970: 36–37
18. Herodotus, *Histories* 2.59.1
19. Sawyer 1996: 59–60
20. Ferguson 1970: 100
21. The largest river in Syria, now Nahr el-Asi.
22. Juvenal, *Satires* 3.60–64, trans. Green 1998: 15
23. Takács 1995: 6
24. Bateman 2000: 36
25. Daniels 1989: 6–8
26. Takács 1995
27. Livy, *Histories* 39.15, trans. Sage 1936: 261
28. Ibid., 39.8, 241–243
29. Suetonius, *Lives: Domitian* 1
30. Dio, *Roman History* 40.47.3
31. Turcan 1996: 87
32. Grant 1971: 36
33. Turcan 1996: 111–112
34. Ibid., 114–116
35. Ibid., 116–118
36. *Britannia* 7 (1996) : 378–379, no. 2
37. Henig 1984: 48

38. Ibid., 114; Johns 1996: 115–118
39. Henig 1984: 113–114

CHAPTER 7: The Death of a Gladiatrix
1. Auguet 1994: 60–61
2. Junkelmann 2000: 69–70
3. Grant 1967: 49
4. Auguet 1994: 180
5. Dio, *Roman History* 78.6
6. Kyle 1998: 158
7. Seneca, *Letters* 93.12
8. Auguet 1994: 215–216
9. Kyle 1998: 159
10. Hope 2000: 95
11. Kyle 1998: 163
12. Toynbee 1971: 49
13. Kyle 1998: 227
14. Wiedemann 1995: 30
15. Kyle 1998: 161
16. Ibid., 225–227
17. Toynbee 1971: 54–55
18. Ibid., 113–116
19. See chapter 4.
20. Hope 2000: 99
21. Hope 1998, 2000
22. Auguet 1994: 180
23. Hope 2000: 103
24. Hope 1998: 183
25. Ferguson 1970: 71–72
26. Ogilvie 1969: 123
27. Henig 1984: 69
28. Toynbee 1971: 63–64
29. Ibid., 43–50

30. Philpott 1991: 48–49
31. Ibid., 192
32. Ibid., 193
33. Toynbee 1971: 44–45

CONCLUSION
1. Pringle 2001: 53
2. Philpott 1991: 195
3. Turcan 1996: 90
4. Juvenal, *Satires* 6.112, trans. Ewigleben 2000: 125

BIBLIOGRAPHY

ANCIENTS SOURCES

Apollonius Rhodius, *Argonautica*. Trans. by R. C. Seaton (1930). Loeb Classical Library. William Heinemann: London.

Julius Caesar, *The Conquest of Gaul*. Trans. by S. A. Handford (rev. ed. 1982). Penguin Classics: London.

Cicero, *Letters to Atticus*. Trans. by E. O. Winstedt (1956). Loeb Classical Library. Harvard University Press: Cambridge.

Cicero, *Tusculan Disputations*. Trans. by J. E. King (1966). Loeb Classical Library. Harvard University Press: Cambridge.

Dio Cassius, *Roman History*. Trans. by E. Cary (1968). Loeb Classical Library. Harvard University Press: Cambridge.

Herodotus, *Histories*

Homer, *The Iliad*

Josephus, *The Jewish War*

Juvenal, *The Sixteen Satires*. Trans. by Peter Green (1998). Penguin Classics: London.

Juvenal, *Satires*. Trans. by G. G. Ramsay (1940). Loeb Classical Library. Harvard University Press: Cambridge.

Livy, *The Early History of Rome*. Trans. by Aubrey de Sélincourt (1971). Penguin Classics: New York.

Livy, *Rome and Italy*. Trans. by Betty Radice (1987). Penguin Classics: Harmondsworth.

Livy, *Histories*. Trans. by Evan T. Sage (1936). Loeb Classical Library. Harvard University Press: Cambridge.

Martial, *Epigrams*. Trans. by Walter C. A. Ker (1968). Loeb Classical Library. Harvard University Press: Cambridge

Martial, *On The Spectacles*. Trans. by Walter C. A. Ker (1968). Loeb Classical Library. Harvard University Press: Cambridge.

Petronius, *Satyricon*. Trans. by Michael Heseltine (1969). Loeb Classical Library. Harvard University Press: Cambridge.

Plato, *Laws*

Pliny the Elder, *Natural History*

Pliny the Younger, *Letters*

Plutarch, *Crassus*

Plutarch, *Isis and Osiris*

Prudentius, *Reply to Symmachus*. Trans. by H. J. Thomson (1953). Loeb Classical Library. Harvard University Press: Cambridge.

Seneca, *Letters*

Statius, *Silvae*

Strabo, *Geography*. Trans. by H. L. Jones (1961). Loeb Classical Library. Harvard University Press: Cambridge.

Suetonius, *The Lives of the Caesars*

Tacitus, *A Dialogue on Oratory*

Tacitus, *The Agricola*. Trans. by H. Mattingly (1970). Penguin Classics: London.

Tacitus, *The Annals of Imperial Rome*. Trans. by Michael Grant (1989). Penguin Classics: London.

Vegetius, *The Epitome of Military Science*. Trans. by N. P. Milner (1996). Liverpool University Press: Liverpool.

Virgil, *The Aeneid*; Trans. by W. F. Jackson Knight (1986). Penguin Classics: London.

WORKS CONSULTED

Allason-Jones, Lindsay

    1989 *Women in Roman Britain*. British Museum Publications: London.

Andrae, Bernard

    1991 The image of the Celts in Etruscan, Greek and Roman art, in *The Celts*, edited by V. Kruta, O. H. Frey, B. Raftery and M. Szabó. Rizzoli International Publications, Inc.: New York. Pp. 61–69.

Auguet, Roland

    1994 *Cruelty and Civilization: The Roman Games*. Barnes & Noble Books: New York.

Balsdon, J.P.V.D.

    1990 *Roman Women: Their History and Habits*. Barnes & Noble Books: New York.

Barber, Bruno, and Jenny Hall

    2000 Digging up the people of Roman London: interpreting evidence from Roman London's cemeteries, in *London Underground: The Archaeology of a City*, edited by Ian Haynes, Harvey Sheldon, and Lesley Hannigan. Oxbow Books: Oxford. Pp. 102–120.

Bateman, Nick

    2000 *Gladiators at the Guildhall: The Story of London's Roman Amphitheater and Medieval Guildhall*. Museum of London Archaeology Service: London.

Bradley, Keith R.

    1986 Wet-nursing at Rome: a study in social relations, in *The Family in Ancient Rome: New Perspectives*, edited by Beryl Rawson. Cornell University Press: Ithaca. Pp. 201–229.

Brothers, A. J.

    1995 "Buildings for entertainment" in *Roman Public Buildings*, edited by Ian M. Barton. University of Exeter Press: Exeter.

Bulfinch, Thomas

    1947 *Bulfinch's Mythology*. Thomas Y. Crowell Co.: New York.

Daniels, Charles

    1989 *Mithras and His Temples on the Wall*. Museum of Antiquities of the University and the Society of Antiquities: Newcastle Upon Tyne.

Davis-Kimball, Jeannine
1997 Warrior women of the Eurasian steppes. *Archaeology* 50(1): 44–48.

Drummond-Murray, James, and Peter Thompson
1998 Did Boudica burn Southwark? The story of the Jubilee Line Extension. *Current Archaeology* 14.2(158): 48–49.

Engels, Donald
1980 The problem of female infanticide in the Greco-Roman world. *Classical Philology* 75: 112–120.

Etienne, Robert
1992 *Pompeii: The Day a City Died*. Trans. by Caroline Palmer. Harry N. Abrams, Inc.: New York.

Evans, John K.
1991 *War, Women and Children in Ancient Rome*. Routledge: London.

Ewigleben, Cornelia
2000 " 'What these women love is the sword': the performers and their audiences" in *Gladiators and Caesars: The Power of Spectacle in Ancient Rome*, edited by Eckart Köhne and Cornelia Ewigleben. University of California Press: Berkeley. Pp. 125–139.

Ferguson, John
1970 *The Religions of the Roman Empire*. Cornell University Press: Ithaca.

Flemming, Rebecca
1999 *Quae corpore quaestum facit*: the sexual economy of female prostitution in the Roman Empire. *Journal of Roman Studies* 89: 38–61.

Fantham, Elaine, Helene Peet Foley, Natalie Boymel Kampen, Sarah B. Pomeroy, and H. A. Shapiro
1994 *Women in the Classical World: Image and Text*. Oxford University Press: Oxford.

Frier, Bruce W.
1999 Roman demography, in *Life, Death, and Entertainment in the Roman Empire*, edited by D. S. Potter and D. J. Mattingly. University of Michigan Press: Ann Arbor. Pp. 85–109.

Futrell, Alison

    1997 *Blood in the Arena: the Spectacle of Roman Power*. University of Texas Press: Austin.

Gardner, Jane F., and Thomas Wiedemann

    1991 *The Roman Household: A Sourcebook*. Routledge: New York.

Giorgi, John

    2000 The plant remains—a summary, in *A Romano-British Cemetery on Watling Street*, edited by Anthony Mackinder. Museum of London Archaeological Service, Archaeology Studies Series 4: 65–66.

Golden, Mark

    1988 Did the ancients care when their children died? *Greece & Rome* 35(2): 152–163.

Grant, Michael

    1967 *Gladiators*. Barnes & Noble Books: New York.

    1971 *Cities of Vesuvius: Pompeii and Herculaneum*. The Macmillan Company: New York.

Hall, Jenny

    1996 The cemeteries of Roman London: a review, in *Interpreting Roman London: Papers in Memory of Hugh Chapman*, edited by Joanna Bird, Mark Hassall, and Harvey Sheldon. Oxbow Monograph 58: 57–84.

Hanson, Ann E.

    1999 The Roman family, in *Life, Death, and Entertainment in the Roman Empire*, edited by D. S. Potter and D. J. Mattingly. University of Michigan Press: Ann Arbor. Pp. 19–66.

Haynes, Ian

    2000 Religion in Roman London, in *London Underground: The Archaeology of a City*, edited by Ian Haynes, Harvey Sheldon, and Lesley Hannigan. Oxbow Books: Oxford. Pp. 85–101.

Henig, Martin

    1984 *Religion in Roman Britain*. St. Martin's Press: New York.

Hope, Valerie M.

    1998 Negotiating identity and status: the gladiators of Roman Nîmes, in *Cultural Identity in the Roman Empire*, edited by Ray Laurence and Joanne Berry. Routledge: London. Pp. 179–195.

2000 Fighting for identity: the funerary commemoration of Italian gladiators, in *The Epigraphic Landscape of Roman Italy*, edited by Alison Cooley. Institute of Classical Studies, School of Advanced Study, University of London: London. Pp. 93–113.

Hornblower, Simon, and Antony Spawforth (Eds.)

1996 *The Oxford Classical Dictionary* (3rd ed.). Oxford University Press: Oxford.

Johns, Catherine

1996 Isis, not Cybele: a bone hairpin from London, in *Interpreting Roman London: Papers in Memory of Hugh Chapman*, edited by Joanna Bird, Mark Hassall, and Harvey Sheldon. Oxbow Monograph 58: 115–118.

Junkelmann, Marcus

2000 "*Familia gladiatoria*: the heroes of the amphitheater" in *Gladiators and Caesars: The Power of Spectacle in Ancient Rome*, edited by Eckart Köhne and Cornelia Ewigleben. University of California Press: Berkeley. Pp. 31–74.

Köhne, Eckart

2000 "Bread and circuses: the politics of entertainment" in *Gladiators and Caesars: The Power of Spectacle in Ancient Rome*, edited by Eckart Köhne and Cornelia Ewigleben. University of California Press: Berkeley. Pp. 8–30.

Kyle, Donald G.

1998 *Spectacles of Death in Ancient Rome*. Routledge: London.

Laurence, Ray

1994 *Roman Pompeii: Space and Society*. Routledge: London

Lefkowitz, Mary R., and Maureen B. Fant

1992 *Women's Life in Greece & Rome: A Sourcebook in Translation*. Johns Hopkins University Press: Baltimore.

Luongo, Giuseppe, Annamaria Perrota, and Claudio Scarpati

1999 The eruption of A.D. 79, in *Pompeii: Life in a Roman Town*, edited by Annamaria Ciarallo and Ernesto De Carolis. Electa: Milan. Pp. 31–33.

Mackinder, Anthony

2000 *A Romano-British Cemetery on Watling Street*. Museum of London

Archaeological Service, Archaeology Studies Series 4.

Nappo, Salvatore

    1998 *Pompeii: A Guide to the Ancient City*. Barnes & Noble Books: New York.

Ogilvie, R. M.

    1969 *The Romans and Their Gods in the Age of Augustus*. W. W. Norton & Company: New York.

Philpott, Robert

    1991 *Burial Practices in Roman Britain: A Survey of Grave Treatment and Furnishing A.D. 43–410*. BAR British Series 219.

Potter, T. W., and Catherine Johns

    1992 *Roman Britain*. British Museum Press: London.

Pringle, Heather.

    2001 Gladiatrix. *Discover* 22(12): 48–55.

Rawson, Beryl

    1986 The Roman family, in *The Family in Ancient Rome: New Perspectives*, edited by Beryl Rawson. Cornell University Press: Ithaca. Pp. 1–57.

Sawyer, Deborah F.

    1996 *Women and Religion in the First Christian Centuries*. Routledge: London.

Sealey, Paul R.

    1997 *The Boudican Revolt Against Rome*. Shire Publications: Princes Risborough.

Sheldon, Harvey

    2000 Roman Southwark, in *London Underground: The Archaeology of a City*, edited by Ian Haynes, Harvey Sheldon, and Lesley Hannigan. Oxbow Books: Oxford. Pp. 121–150.

Shelton, Jo-Ann

    1998 *As the Romans Did*. Oxford University Press: Oxford.

Stroh, Wilfried

    2000 "Give us your applause!" in *Gladiators and Caesars: The Power of Spectacle in Ancient Rome*, edited by Eckart Köhne and Cornelia Ewigleben. University of California Press: Berkeley. Pp. 103–124.

Swan, Vivien G.

   1988 *Pottery in Roman Britain* (4th edition). Shire Archaeology: Princes
      Risborough.

Takács, Sarolta A.

   1995 *Isis and Sarapis in the Roman World*. E. J. Brill: Leiden.

Toynbee, J.M.C.

   1971 *Death and Burial in the Roman World*. Johns Hopkins University
      Press: Baltimore.

Turcan, Robert

   1996 *The Cults of the Roman Empire*. Blackwell: Oxford.

Vesley, Mark

   1998 Gladiatorial training for girls in the *collegia iuvenum* of the Roman
      Empire. *Echos du Monde Classique* 42(17): 85–93.

Veyne, Paul

   1992 The Roman Empire, in *A History of Private Life, Volume 1: From
      Pagan Rome to Byzantium*, edited by Paul Veyne (trans. by Arthur
      Goldhammer). Harvard University Press: Cambridge. Pp. 5–233.

Wardle, Andrea

   2000 Funerary rites, burial practices and belief, in *A Romano-British
      Cemetery on Watling Street*, by Anthony Mackinder. Museum of Lon-
      don Archaeological Service, Archaeology Studies Series 4: 27–30.

Ward-Perkins, John, and Amanda Claridge

   1978 *Pompeii AD 79*. Museum of Fine Arts: Boston.

Webster, Graham

   1999 *Boudica: The British Revolt Against Rome AD 69*. Routledge: London.

Wiedemann, Thomas

   1995 *Emperors & Gladiators*. Routledge: London.

Will, Elizabeth Lyding

   1979 Women in Pompeii. *Archaeology* 32(5): 34–43.

Witt, R. E.

   1971 *Isis in the Ancient World*. Johns Hopkins University Press: Balti-
      more.

INDEX

Amy Zoll has a master's degree in Roman archaeology from the University of Durham. She is currently pursuing a Ph.D. at the University of Pennsylvania. She has worked at Roman sites in England and France (in addition to two seasons at Pompeii). She has had several articles published in academic journals. *Gladiatrix* is her first full-length work.